Breaking Bad Habits of
Race and Gender

Breaking Bad Habits of Race and Gender

Transforming Identity in Schools

Sarah Marie Stitzlein

ROWMAN & LITTLEFIELD PUBLISHERS, INC.
Lanham • Boulder • New York • Toronto • Plymouth, UK

ROWMAN & LITTLEFIELD PUBLISHERS, INC.

Published in the United States of America
by Rowman & Littlefield Publishers, Inc.
A wholly owned subsidary of The Rowman & Littlefield Publishing Group, Inc.
4501 Forbes Boulevard, Suite 200, Lanham, Maryland 20706
www.rowmanlittlefield.com

Estover Road
Plymouth PL6 7PY
United Kingdom

British Library Cataloguing in Publication Information Available

Library of Congress Cataloging-in-Publication Data:

Stitzlein, Sarah Marie, 1979-
 Breaking bad habits of race and gender : transforming identity in schools / Sarah Marie
Stitzlein.
     p. cm.
 Includes bibliographical references and index.
 ISBN-13: 978-0-7425-6358-2 (cloth : alk. paper)
 ISBN-10: 0-7425-6358-8 (cloth : alk. paper)
 ISBN-13: 978-0-7425-6359-9 (pbk : alk. paper)
 ISBN-10: 0-7425-6359-6 (pbk : alk. paper)
 eISBN-13: 978-0-7425-6568-5
 eISBN-10: 0-7425-6568-8

 1. Discrimination in education—United States. 2. Sex discrimination in education—
United States. 3. Educational equalization—United States. I. Title.
 LC212.2S75 2008
 379.2'60973—dc22   2008019229

Printed in the United States of America

♾™ The paper used in this publication meets the minimum requirements of American
National Standard for Information Sciences—Permanence of Paper for Printed Library
Materials, ANSI/NISO Z39.48-1992.

Contents

Acknowledgments

I would be remiss to not acknowledge my recent colleagues who assisted in the making of this book: Nicholas Burbules, Walter Feinberg, Thomas Schwandt, Bryan Warnick, and Craig West. Much of my appreciation, however, extends in a different direction. I would like to thank the many teachers and professors who have shown me how education can be truly transformative and who have attuned me to the hope that lies within classrooms around the globe. In particular, I would like to thank my earliest teachers, my parents, Gary and Diana Stitzlein, not only for teaching me the three Rs but also for teaching me how to appreciate life's simple pleasures—a good laugh, the beauty of the Midwest countryside, and the joys of farm life. Thanks also to my third-grade teacher and longtime pen pal, Jennifer Richards, for sharing her passion for writing with me and for showing me that a teacher's commitment to a student does not end on the last day of class. Thanks to Kathleen Knight Abowitz for opening the door to the field of philosophy of education for me and, more importantly, for walking through it with me as a mentor and friend. Thanks to Cris Mayo for making me so (un)comfortable once I arrived inside. Finally, a special appreciation to Richard Momeyer for recognizing many years ago what an incredible journey education is for me and for always knowing how to guide me through it.

Chapter One

Introduction

September 2006 brought the beginning of an ongoing battle in the small town of Jena, Louisiana—a battle that has reminded many that we have a long way to go in achieving racial equality and alleviating racial tensions in our schools. Sounding much like a story from the pre–Civil Rights era, the events at Jena High have unfolded in deeply troubling ways. At the beginning of the school year, a new black student requested permission to sit under a tree in the school yard that was previously exclusively occupied by whites. The next morning, white students hung three nooses from the tree. Tensions quickly escalated, as the white students received only a minor reprimand for what was dubbed a simple "prank" by the administration. Black students rallied together under the tree until the police were called.

Over the next few months, skirmishes erupted on and off school grounds between white and black students. In November, part of the school was burned to the ground. In December, one white student, Justin Barker, began to taunt black classmate, Robert Bailey, who had been threatened with a gun and insulted by a white man the previous evening. Bailey and five of his friends broke into a fight with Barker, who sustained superficial injuries and went out to a social event after being released from medical care a few hours later. Nonetheless, Bailey and his five friends—now known in the media as the "Jena 6"—were brought up on charges of second-degree attempted murder and aggravated assault. On July 31, 2007, Mychal Ball, the first defendant to be tried, was found guilty by an all-white jury of the reduced charges of aggravated battery and conspiracy. These convictions were later overturned because Ball was tried as an adult and not properly tried as a minor. He now stands to be retried in December 2007.

As the fate of Mychal and his friends remains to be seen, the school is divided over the situation, and the rest of the country is left facing the reality that race problems with serious implications continue to plague our schools.[1]

1

While the tree that started it all has since been chopped down to prevent future problems, more serious changes need to be made at that school and others.

Teachers and students in classrooms encounter difficult situations everyday arising from differences between genders or races or from bias and hostility that relate to those differences. Often classroom events are divided by gender and racial lines, lacking communication, cooperative learning across difference, and integration of all classroom members. In the most drastic cases, such as the case in Jena, these situations erupt into overt conflict or violence. In other cases, they go largely unnoted, typically inflicting harm on minority students without even being recognized by those in the racial or gender majority. Such incidents reveal that despite equality legislation and formal desegregation, racial and gender problems persist. These events pose substantial restraints on the achievement of educational equality, student ability to explore nontraditional ways of being, proliferation of diversity, and student development of democratic ways of living.

Many parents, administrators, teachers, and educational scholars struggle to interpret these situations. Some claim that problematic classroom exchanges cannot be based on gender or racial difference because children, especially in the early years of schooling, are "color blind" and do not even recognize difference. As will become evident in the classroom events depicted throughout this book, this is most certainly not the case. Continuing to propel such myths supports a dominant cover-up of racism and sexism, denies the harmful effects of these systems on children, and overlooks the fact that racism and sexism can spring from kids themselves. Children exhibit considerable knowledge of racial and gender difference as well as social implications of these differences. As early as age three, 40 percent of children are able to distinguish gender even when some traditional visual cues are distorted and are aware of gendered guidelines for dress and behavior.[2] Knowledge of difference grows in complexity as students age. One poignant example of student recognition of both difference and the tenuous relations between different groups is evident in an exchange a teacher reports with one of her high school students:

> "They say all people from Europe are supposed to be white, right? And all the people from Africa are supposed to be black, right? And all the people—Indians are supposed to be red, right? And all the Asian people are supposed to be yellow, right? These are the colors people are givin' 'em. So it seems just like sports—they put 'em all in teams, like categories," he says. "*Yes!* And why do they put 'em into teams?" I ask. "To make 'em compete!" he finishes.[3]

Many educational philosophers and social theorists have attempted to explain problematic school situations, often with recourse to theories of racism and sexism. These theories typically hold that racism and sexism are based on beliefs and values that assert either explicitly or implicitly that one group is inferior to another by virtue of biology, social position, historical role, religious doctrine, or other similar hierarchical guidelines. Typically, females and nonwhite people are viewed as inferior, resulting in dehumanization and domination of the members of these groups as well as the groups as a whole. Many theorists have attempted to analyze classroom conflicts between differing genders and races in terms of the biased beliefs of one group toward another. Following that train of thought, they have suggested that teachers and students can combat racism and sexism by willfully working against injustice, often by changing biased beliefs.

Recent scholarship on racism and sexism, however, suggests that rarely is racism or sexism a consistent set of beliefs held by one person toward another group. Instead, each is contradictory and shifting.[4] Racism and sexism are not sets of beliefs and values external to a person who comprehensively adopts and employs them at will. Rather, they internally form us in complex and conflicting ways that typically operate below the conscious level of belief. This includes shaping the ways in which we habitually enact our own races and genders and interact with those who are different from ourselves. Understanding racism and sexism in the traditional way has not fully explained embodied interactions between different people, including the staying force of these prejudices. Traditional theories have also offered only limited theoretical tools for social justice educators. These views have led to ineffective antibias curricula and pedagogies that abstractly teach about difference and values of equality without promoting difference to play out on the bodies of students and guiding students through moments of encountering difference.

In this book, I offer a more nuanced analysis of classroom situations inhibited by racial and gender difference by investigating how these events arise from rigid habits of living one's race and gender or rigid habits of responding to the races and genders of others. I recount and probe many actual classroom events witnessed by myself, other teachers, or educational researchers that depict racial and gender interaction. This book adopts, in part, the philosophical perspective of pragmatism. Gregory Fernando Pappas rightly points out pragmatists' concerns with specific contexts when investigating racism and, I would add, sexism. He asks,

> Can a philosophy committed to sensitivity to context really engage in a general account of racism? Strictly speaking there is no general problem of racism but specific problems suffered by particular individuals or communities. The racism experienced by blacks in the North may be different in its conditions than the one experienced by blacks in the South. Even among a particular community there may be important changes in the problem across time. Inquiring about the racist or racism in general is a dangerous abstraction.[5]

It is because of the concerns with specific contexts that I begin with, adhere to, and return repeatedly to actual classroom situations as I attempt to flesh out a more broad understanding of racism and sexism. Staying true to these situations reminds me of their nuance and their variations, thereby complicating my larger theory and urging me to make specific recommendations for dealing with certain circumstances. These situations also reveal that better understanding and alleviating problems of identity is likely inherent in these events themselves rather than contained solely within theoretical exploration.

Drawing on these events, I consider some of the successful and unsuccessful ways in which students have dealt with sticky situations of race and gender. Emerging out of analysis of their efforts, I suggest that when students learn to inhabit their genders and races more flexibly, some problematic interactions between races and genders might be prevented and, in the long run, social hierarchies might be positively transformed. I tease out an apparent contradiction in the popular use of the term "habit" by suggesting that habit can actually be reconceived as a flexible, intelligent way of enacting identity rather than a stagnant way of maintaining traditional roles. I argue that schools can innovatively cultivate flexible habits within students in ways that increase the students' agency in shaping their own lives and transforming societal and classroom moments of impasse. I paradoxically use "habit," then, both to explain why race and gender problems have not been more fully ameliorated and to show how they can be.

Many decades ago, a key figure in educational philosophy, John Dewey, presented a useful and complex account of habit in his book *Human Nature and Conduct*. He spent little time, however, considering how his concept of habit is relevant to the embodiment of race and gender. In chapter 2, I describe and analyze Dewey's notion of habit from both the perspectives of education and identity. When habit is understood as constitutive of race and gender as well as responses to race and gender, Dewey's notion of habit can be extended in intriguing ways. I draw on Dewey's philosophy to interpret the classroom situations provided in terms of the race and gender habits of students as well as their ways of responding to students whose races and genders differ from their own.

Employing Dewey's theory of transaction, I depict students as beings who continually transact with their environment. This transaction entails a fairly thoroughgoing but not entirely complete social construction of human subjects. The child is brought into being through transactions with objective conditions, cultural norms, and institutions that develop habitual ways of acting that shape the child into standard appearances and activities, including socially defined race and gender. Not only do our habits play key roles in the formation of our identities, but they are the meaningful lived experience of being race and gendered as well as our responses to the identities of others.

Rather than a merely psychological understanding of habit, Dewey provides an account of habits as both bodily comportment and nonmaterial predispositions to act or sensitivities to certain ways of being. Following Dewey, I contend that habits become problematic when they grow stagnant, when they demand continual repetitions that fail to keep up with the changing world, or when they prevent fruitful transactions between people. I locate examples of these failures in actual classrooms, explaining how gender and racial violence and disconnect results from rigid habits of identity, particularly as they play out through bodily activity. Insofar as schools are tasked with developing innovative, dynamic students who can work together to solve social problems, including problems of hierarchical identity, these potential pitfalls of habit are central concerns of education.

In chapter 3, I defend my claim that race is defined and inculcated by habit through employing Dewey's notion of habit to offer an analysis of the historical formation and maintenance of race. Dewey, a man personally committed to antiracist causes, largely overlooked race within his philosophical works and failed to suggest ways for dealing with race in his pedagogical writings. Indeed, while race and racial problems plagued society during his time, the troubling absence of these issues within his writing is indicative of a larger failure of pragmatism. As Bill Lawson rightly reflects on the tradition, "If a Martian were to come down to America and look at the American pragmatist tradition, they would never know that there was slavery, Jim Crow, lynching, discrimination, segregation in the history of America."[6] Chapter 3 redresses these inexcusable oversights. It overtly discusses race and breaches the topic by beginning with the discourse that Dewey and other pragmatists valorized and analyzed at length: science. Through historical analysis of primary sources within early modern science, I offer a genealogy of race as it was conceived and studied within science to show that, while race appears to be a natural essence or surface-level trait, it is actually a result of scientific focus on habitual activity. I concentrate on the history of science because this tradition has had the most overwhelming and lasting impact on popular present-day self-identifications and group interactions—including beliefs of natural distinction and hierarchy that carry over into the classroom. Additionally, I highlight this field because of its uniquely precarious position of having once championed race and now proclaiming its nonexistence. These changes are noteworthy for my larger social and educational efforts to better understand and rework race.

Through historical analysis of primary sources within early modern science, I reveal how race was determined and tested not only on the basis of surface-level differences, like skin color, but most notably by the habitual activities of bodies. Such an investigation, when paired with an account of science's corresponding institutions of economic and meritocratic hierarchy, exposes the political interests served through racial designation by habit. Moreover, my analysis suggests not only *that* race is a social construction, as many before me have claimed, but also *how* and *why* it is. The historical analysis concludes with a consideration of the contemporary lived experience of race, including the corporeal phenomenon of inhabiting race—of being *in* one's habits. Such inhabitation can shed light on why racial classifications persist despite recent advances in genetics having debunked the validity of race in the late twentieth century. Moreover, in the context of racial hierarchy in the classroom, this analysis suggests that even in the absence of institutional and attitudinal racism, racial tension will remain as long as race continues to be inhabited discretely and inflexibly.

My account of race in terms of habit shares many similarities with contemporary theorizations of gender. Over the past decade, several poststructural theorists, especially those associated with feminism, have begun to theorize how bodies materialize and are maintained as gendered. Judith Butler, in particular, has offered a provocative portrait of this process through her description of gender performativity. I consider this theory and its implications for classroom identity problems in chapter 4.

Discursive performativity, for Butler, both describes the gendered body and brings it into being. For Butler, gender is a ritual one performs continuously through the way one does (or does not) appear, speak, and act. Gender is an effect rather than an inherent trait. It is produced by a series of repetitions of norms and cultural constraints that become naturalized over time. The norms repeated entail exclusions of different types and ways of being in order to maintain discretely defined, coherent categories of gender. Because these norms are repeated in the process of developing and maintaining gendered identity, hierarchies of being are constructed that privilege certain consistent and culturally acceptable ways of being and that render others unintelligible. The continuous performance of gender makes it appear natural and primary, covering over its constructed source.

Understood as such, gender and its inherent exclusions lead Butler to promote acts of subversion that reveal gender as performative rather than natural. She also endorses linguistic adventures that teeter on the realm of the unspeakable, thereby exposing the arbitrary and problematic line defining gender acceptability. These acts occur, seemingly spontaneously, through an agent who redeploys the power of the cultural norms and linguistic structures that constitute him or her. Thereby, Butler, through her description of the subject's ability to vary the repetition of norms as gender is performed, offers a provocative notion of political agency—one bearing significant educational implications, which I explain.

Butler's theory of performativity and the political goals that follow from it may be helpful for understanding classroom situations marked by gender and racial stagnation. As primarily a linguistic rather than an educational philosopher, Butler has not been overtly tasked with analyzing schools as a central location of learning gender. I resituate Butler's notions of the constructed subject, political agency, and performativity within the school, thereby investigating the ways in which her work is and is not helpful for addressing classroom dilemmas. I consider how the process of gender identification arises explicitly in schools, and I locate the process of and subversive response to gendering as an educational issue. Butler does not see gender as centrally a problem to be addressed and worked out in schools, nor does she acknowledge the potential political impact of pliable youth engaged in collective struggle within the world's largest social institution. Neither does Butler explicitly provide pedagogical tools for social justice educators to address the problems of gender sedimentation and hierarchy within classroom walls. I aim to redress these oversights in ways that strive primarily to offer a more complex and complete understanding of racial and gender problems and secondarily to contribute to current scholarship on Butler.

In chapter 5, I develop an account of gender formation, maintenance, and change. This account grows out of, supplements, and surpasses that of both Butler and Dewey. While retaining Butler's insight into the constructed nature of subjectivity, the problematic effects of gender sedimentation, the complex notion of agency as within power rather than acting against it, and some of her goals for change, I reground her work within a central event of education—the development of habits—and within the concrete instances of failed race and gender interaction within schools evident in the examples I provide. Drawing on the work of Dewey, I construct an understanding of habit that supplements and extends Butler's work on performativity, draws parallels between the inhabiting of race and gender, and provides new insight into classroom identity conflicts.

Building off of Dewey's discussion of reworking habit through inquiry and experiment when problematic situations arise, I craft the crux of my argument: the notion of flexible habit. While growing out of but significantly differing from both Butler and Dewey, flexible habit suggests that habits themselves can and should be held tentatively and with intelligent foresight into future situations so as to avoid and confront problems of stagnation and impasse, particularly fixed, hierarchical experiences of race and gender. Flexible habits offer us a platform for acting in the world by enabling political agency and do not pin us down into predetermined ways of being. Like Butler's gender performativity, flexible habits are a doing, but when made intelligent or plastic in educational settings, they support the doing of gender differently. They allow and invite the variation

on repetition that Butler desires and the educative growth Dewey seeks. Moreover, engaging flexible habits can enable students and teachers to enact the
agency necessary for reworking classroom identity conflicts. Finally, and most
importantly, my notion of flexible habit suggests concrete ways in which habits
can challenge the apparent naturalness of identity categories and open up new
ways of being. Through transaction and the reworking of habit, objective
changes to the environment, particularly to those institutions that preserve rigid
identity distinction, including schools, may also be made.

Chapter 6 returns to a key location of habit formation and a space of racial
and gender problems that I identified at the outset: the classroom. In hopes of
guiding social justice educators, I offer concrete suggestions for how a classroom focused on flexible habits might look and how it might deal with race
and gender conflict, including the very exclusionary practice of identity itself.
I revisit the classroom narratives and teacher anecdotes I have depicted
throughout the book in order to depict how those situations might be better
understood and transformed through the development of flexible habits. By
describing social and political change in terms of a practice teachers currently
conduct—the cultivation of habits—I am able to offer pedagogical suggestions that are compatible with current teacher practice while simultaneously
strengthening teachers' understanding of hierarchical identity formation and
providing new tools for social transformation. I point teachers toward con-
ducting historical analysis with their classes that reveal the ways in which
habits have defined races and genders and the ways they continue to affect the
perception of and response to identity categories. I argue that teachers should
create realistic scenarios that urge students to examine their own habits as
well as the ways in which the construction of their races and genders relies on
and sustains the oppression of other groups.

Furthermore, I envision the classroom as a supportive space of experiment—a place where students can enact race and gender differently and in
ways that destabilize normative traditional identities. I suggest classroom activities that bolster flexible habits and the self-reflection and willingness to
change that they require. I also describe how students can engage in larger political struggles to end identity hierarchy and to change the social institutions
that support these practices.

Finally, I draw on the emerging fields of critical race theory and whiteness
studies to consider how white students may be made uncomfortable with the
ways in which their habits typically define the norm against which others are
judged as different. Those students may come to understand and work against
their complicity in the oppression of other racial groups. I consider whether
races remain as discrete groupings as transaction occurs. Taking account of
potential changes in races over time, I consider the ethical imperative to pre-

vent the preservation of whiteness as privilege. I also use this literature to consider how my suggestions, particularly as a white person, may presuppose white ways of being, white privilege, and white ease when traversing the educational world.

This is a project that focuses on habit and, by doing so, allows us to better understand identity. Identity comes about as habit that is repetitively enacted, and cultural and normative terms are used to label certain patterns of enactment. When these patterns are similarly displayed by many people, those people are defined as an identity group, such as women or Latinos. Recognizing identity as such a product allows me to offer a unique explanatory concept via flexible habit. It shows that when habits become no longer easily pinned down or encompassed by identity categories because of their continuous variation, the very notion of identity as a normative description of distinctly separated groups is debunked. Schools, as cultivators of habits, are exceptionally capable of fostering this type of valuable social, political, and educational work.

NOTES

1. Wade Goodwyn, "Beating Charges Split Louisiana Town along Racial Lines," *All Things Considered,* National Public Radio, July 30, 2007; Amy Goodman, "Justice for the Jena Six," *Aspen Daily News*, July 31, 2007.

2. Sandra Lipsitz Bem, "Genital Knowledge and Gender Constancy in Preschool Children," *Child Development* 60, no. 3 (1989): 649–62; Robyn M. Holmes, *How Young Children Perceive Race* (Thousand Oaks, Calif.: Sage, 1995), 35.

3. Mica Pollock, *Colormute: Race Talk Dilemmas in an American School* (Princeton, N.J.: Princeton University Press, 2004), 39–40.

4. Paul Connolly, *Racism, Gender Identities, and Young Children* (London: Routledge, 1998), 10–11.

5. Gregory Fernando Pappas, "Distance, Abstraction, and the Role of the Philosopher in the Pragmatic Approach to Racism," in *Pragmatism and the Problem of Race*, ed. Bill E. Lawson and Donald F. Koch (Bloomington: Indiana University Press, 2004), 24.

6. Bill E. Lawson, "Afterword: A Conversation between Cornel West and Bill E. Lawson," in Lawson and Koch, *Pragmatism and the Problem of Race*, 225.

Chapter Two

Deweyan Habits

One day while teaching at a preschool, I saw one of the students' favorite games in a new light. My grandmother fondly recalls playing "house" as a child. Children today continue to enjoy role-playing family members and pretending to go about everyday life in a make-believe house. Typically in my classroom, this was a game most frequented by girls. Often, however, a stray boy would wander over to the "house" and proudly take on the role of father. It was not until the day that I witnessed a boy request and flawlessly assume the role of "mother" that I began to think more deeply about this game. I began to wonder how children learn what actions and behaviors are appropriate for various gendered members of a family. How do they know what to say in order to become a "sister" or a "father"? In the case of the young male "mother," I was pushed to consider what gender boundaries are and how children can convincingly cross them through performing their own genders differently.

More than eighty years ago, when my grandmother was playing "house," American pragmatist philosopher John Dewey produced his seminal work on human individual and social activity, *Human Nature and Conduct*. As Dewey considered the formation and assessment of moral activity in this book, he challenged many claims that dominated the field of psychology in the mid-twentieth century and some of which continue to be upheld today. He issued a view of human conduct that posed an intimate and inseparable connection between the human mind and body as well as between the individual human and his or her environment. This view of human conduct—of the ways in which children learn how to behave—helps explain a game as simple as "house" but also relations as complex as racism and sexism today.

Dewey's notion of habit was central to this work. Highlighted within a piece on moral conduct, his discussion of habit, while complex and nuanced, was restricted in scope and application. In this chapter and the next, I begin

11

to elucidate and analyze Dewey's notion of habit not with explicit respect to human morality but rather in terms of its suitability for understanding the enactment of and response to race and gender. Dewey, a founding member of the National Association for the Advancement of Colored People, wrote little on race, though he was clearly concerned about the status and well-being of black racial minorities in the United States. He did not see that one of his major contributions, the philosophical exegesis of habit, could be an important tool for better understanding racial identity and race relations, especially as they play out in schools. I pick up here where Dewey left off, laying out his understanding of habit in this chapter, followed by a historical look at the relationship between race and habit in chapter 3 and gender and habit in chapter 4.

STUDENTS AS ORGANISMS ENGAGED IN TRANSACTION

Understanding students and all people who are raced and gendered begins, for Dewey, with understanding people as organisms. While "organism" may sound like a cold, technical term used by contemporary scientists who study small samples of organic life under microscopes, Dewey used the term in an entirely different way. For Dewey, "organism" expresses a complex, socially situated, embodied being who engages in multifaceted and reciprocal exchanges with the world around it. Dewey expressed the complexity of these beings by referring to them as "body–minds."[1]

Attempting to trouble Descartes's philosophical mind–body dualism and the historic (and often even contemporary) separation of mind and body popular in psychological studies, Dewey's "body–mind" expresses a nonreductive continuum, with each term used independently only as functional distinctions in certain contexts. In some regards, the body element is one continuous with nature—a local, organic being that is maintained through daily activity and that struggles for its own preservation. Mind emerges from the body when the physical aspects of one's self are engaged in wider activity. It is composed of the consequences of and reflections on interacting with the world, thereby representing the meaning and history of embodied living. Even as mind emerges, it retains traces of the body that can be stripped only at the expense of genuine meaning. Likewise, mind impacts the body, altering its position and way of being in the world. Both mind and body, together as a continuum, occur in specific, contextualized instances as a happening, with spatial, temporal, and mental axes.

Implied from Dewey's own suggestion that many philosophical concepts would be better understood as verbs rather than nouns, "body" may make more sense as the verb or gerund "bodying."[2] This is especially true given that Dewey understood bodies as centers of activity with both mental and physical components. As activity, the body can never be simply a static, physical substance summed up by a noun.

Organisms, according to Dewey, are formed through the process of transaction. Transaction is an ongoing activity where the body–mind balances its well-being with the constantly changing environment. While "environment" for Dewey includes an array of organic, social, and objective conditions, "there is no such thing as an environment in general; there are specific changing objects and events."[3] While broad in scope, then, environment always refers to the intricate context at a specific moment. Transaction may entail the organism adapting to alterations in the environment, or the organism may find it necessary or beneficial to transform the environment to meet its own needs. Transaction is an active and ongoing process of exchange and readjustment between the organism and the environment, whose beginnings and endings are only relative to specific events and purposes.

Transaction is both the way one interacts with the world and the way one comes into being. While Dewey at times appears to uphold a belief in substance metaphysics,[4] reading his account of transaction through a poststructural lens and with an emphasis on the *process* of transaction suggests that there is no organism or essence that exists prior to transaction. Instead, transaction brings the organism into being. It shapes the body, behavior, and knowledge, thereby producing a recognizable person. Transaction molds an otherwise indistinguishable organic mass into culturally coherent ways of being by instilling typical modes of movement, communication, and appearance. These define the being as human and often bear cultural and moral significance, including racial and gender distinction. In turn, the organism performs the conditions of recognizability in ways that both incorporate and alter its environment. Transaction puts the process first, as opposed to interaction, which assumes a previously existing, independent subject who engages with a world distinct and separate from it. Transaction proposes that distinctions between organism and environment arise from this process rather than pre-date it, as though metaphysical givens.[5] Finally, transaction is a continuous process that subjects must continue in order to maintain their status in the world as living, acting, efficacious beings. They must continually transact so that they remain humans worthy of attention and so that they can produce changes in their environment. Transaction is necessary for the maintenance of human life, and fruitful transaction is at the heart of living well.

Transaction is an ongoing series of reciprocal events between two inseparable entities, where each intricately affects and is affected by the other. For Dewey, this occurs between the mental and physical in the body–mind and between the organism and its surroundings. Bodies and their environments are transactionally coconstituted—composing and affecting one another in ways that, at times, render them inseparable or indistinguishable. This concept challenges us to rethink our assumptions about the discreteness of bodies and their surroundings. It pushes us to consider Donna Haraway's provocative question, "Why should our bodies end at the skin, or include at best other beings encapsulated by skin?"[6] A philosophical investigation of transaction calls into question the fixed boundary between the body and its environment, suggesting that each may be permeated by the other. As activities engaging with the world, bodies are vulnerable to being shaped and constituted by the cultural dictates and other people they encounter in such endeavors and vice versa. Indeed, transaction even calls into question the distinction between interior and exterior of the body, challenging us to rethink the connotation of "*em*bodiment" as being contained within a skin, for the activities of being extend beyond its casing. Organisms' distinctions from the world and each other are blurred by virtue of their coconstitution with their surroundings.

Each organism—each student—will react differently to the environment because of his or her unique history and personality. As children transact with some constant and overwhelming cultural forces, however, their responses will often be similar. As I spell out more clearly in the following two chapters, children often transact with institutions and cultural definitions of race and gender in ways that produce similar results in the ways children understand and interact with their world as well as the ways in which their bodies become shaped and identified within it. Transaction can be a conservative process of exchange that perpetuates normative environmental conditions, including race and gender. These transactions can be necessary parts of developing a coherent sense of self that is efficacious in a world where humans are demarcated by race and gender. But the relations that give rise to race and gender can also problematically separate or hierarchically organize groups and individuals, hindering fruitful or ethical transaction between them. As we will see, transaction can also work to change these problematic conditions and, hence, their effects on student body–minds.

IMPULSE

For Dewey, a key player in the process of transaction is impulse. Impulses, or instincts (as he sometimes interchangeably refers to them), are unlearned activities, typically appearing as early as birth. These may include the way a newborn searches for a breast to suckle or the tendency of a man to wince and quickly draw away from an object that pricks him. Dewey conjectured that people across cultures and continents often have similar impulses. He rightly notes, however, that it is the meaning assigned to them, their ability to be productive when intermixed with social tools, and their modification through interaction with the environment that vary from one person to the next. For example, the man's impulse may acquire meanings of pain and prevention of harm, rendering his action significant when witnessed or discussed by others. The simple act of recoiling without his reflection or the observation of others is largely meaningless. The use or act of the impulse may vary. One man may draw on this experience to fashion padding for his skin that prevents future pricks, while another may hone his skills of agility so that he can more quickly escape future pricks before serious damage is done. "In short," Dewey claims, "the *meaning* of native activities is not native; it is acquired. It depends upon interaction with a matured social medium."[7] In some sense, then, the status of impulses as native is, at best, ephemeral and, at worst, a misnomer.

Nonetheless, for Dewey, impulses are bursts of energy, typically taking the form of demands for action or objects that can bring about action. Impulses try to find opportunities where power can be enacted. Employing a Foucauldian notion of power proves useful here in rescuing Dewey from what, at times, appears to be a belief in the wielding of power from without. For, in some cases, Dewey's description of this process seems to uphold power as an external social tool to be acquired, grasped, and deployed at will by an agent. Impulses might more appropriately be understood as drawing out or directing power that is already circulating within the subject and redeploying it in terms of the constitutive power structures that enable being. This sense is evident within Dewey's description of instinct: "It is not so much a demand for power as search for an opportunity to use a power already existing."[8]

For Dewey, there is always a waiting pool of impulses that have not yet come into play. They can do so suddenly on their own, they can play out intelligently and gradually, or they can be suppressed and tucked away. Dewey, in his educational theory, favors impulses that are investigated and gradually played out. Dewey argues that traditionally conservative customs avoid and suppress impulses because they are seen as threatening. Opposingly, he insists that impulses can be taken up as fruitful agents of change. Because of this, he targets the classroom as a space for inquiring into one's impulses, their potential meaning, and how they might be constructively put to use. Dewey envisions impulses as a fount of ingenuity and innovation and attempts to harness them through intelligent inquiry and specified purposes. He believes that impulses can work against established customs and can constitute an individuality within the bearer of the impulse that demarcates him or

her from others. Impulses strike out in new directions but always do so, according to Dewey, with the goal of restoring unified action between the organism and its environment.

HABIT

The Deweyan notion of habit grows out of Dewey's account of impulse, his
understanding of how thought works, and his ideas on which ways of being
are problematic.

Habits, Corporeality, and Commonality

Impulses, in Dewey's view, spring from the individual. They become social
when assigned meaning or when they are organized by habits in light of situations, which necessarily include the environment and other people. Habits,
unlike impulse, are acquired ways of being that are formed through interaction with social institutions and cultural norms as well as the organizing force
of intelligent inquiry. While habits are acquired throughout life and often
within family settings, schools instill or refine the majority of one's lasting
habits. Within school grounds, children watch, imitate, and interact with others. They also learn about socially acceptable behaviors and common activities. Both these direct and indirect teachings form habits in children.

All too often, from rationalizations for why children play "house" to aims
of curriculum development, schools view children as miniature adults or
adults-in-the-making. Because of this, they try to instill typical adult habits
into children, believing that those habits will best socialize them, prepare
them for the workforce, and help them get by in the world. Unfortunately,
however, those adult habits tend to shore up traditional ways of being. In the
United States, this means, in part, preserving a status quo of racism and sexism. Children are not taught to investigate the appropriateness of those habits
or to see schools as a place where injustices are replicated.[9]

Habits also arise through the culmination and processing of impulses.
Habits assemble impulses into patterns or styles of being in the world that one
largely performs effortlessly and without conscious reflection. In Dewey's
words, "All habits are demands for certain kinds of activity; and they constitute the self. In any intelligible sense of the word will they *are* will."[10] There
is no complete person behind the habit who is completely divested from
habits and can choose which habit to enact and when. People do not use
habits at will because they do not preexist them. "The use itself *is* the habit,
and 'we are the habit.'"[11] Dewey, here sounding as though a forerunner of

poststructural theory on subjectivity and performativity, depicts habit as simultaneously produced, performed, and constitutive. Moreover, the "we" he describes are not fixed beings but rather subjects in the process of becoming.

Habits take varying form as skills, dispositions, ways of communicating, sensitivities, modes of response, gestures, or other bodily comportment. Habits can be routine and mechanical skills or adeptness that enable people to operate in the world with ease. Most people experience these types of habits each day: walking, talking, and driving, for example. They are abilities that we come to perform so effortlessly over time that they require little, if any, conscious thought. Indeed, if these activities were suddenly to overwhelm our conscious thoughts, we would no longer be able to carry them out smoothly and efficiently. I recall driving one day and being told by a friend to focus my eyes at a certain distance ahead of me on the road in order to ensure that I did not swerve back and forth in my lane. My efforts at driving soon became so belabored on one aspect of my activity that I ignored oncoming cars in my peripheral vision. When another car approached a stop sign perpendicular to the road I was traveling, I saw it at the last moment, was uncharacteristically startled, and overcorrected my steering in a moment of unnecessary panic. The ease with which I usually drove was disrupted because my conscious thoughts were suddenly consumed with focusing my eyes in a particular way.

Habits often take corporeal form—as bodily comportment or gesture. As I show in the following chapters, these corporeal habits may exhibit culturally defined race or gender insofar as these categories tend to be identified by (or, more precisely, arise through) proclivities of individuals to act or appear in certain stereotypical ways. A teenage boy, for example, may take long strides, proudly hold his head high, and confidently order the other players to take their positions when he makes his way to the center of the football field. Past experience and cultural dictates may suggest that these are appropriate, effective activities and are distinctly masculine—differing from the school yard activities of girls who may chat in small groups or play on the swings. Such corporeal habits are even more evident when they are exaggerated by children playing "house." The children overdo their gendered portrayals of mothers, for example, by excessive talking with their hands or continually offering a soothing touch to others in the house.

Essential to these corporeal habits, for Dewey, is an understanding of habit as a predisposition to act or a sensitivity to ways of being rather than an inclination to repeat identical acts or content precisely. Annette, an adolescent girl whom we will later see is revered by boys on the playground, may tend to stand defiantly in the face of the boy who hits and kicks her. But she may vary this stance from one instance to the next—putting her hands on her hips in one case or putting her fists out in front of her in another. The key point of her habit of defiance is not her precise hand placement or movement but her predisposition to stand up against the bullying boy.

Habits often make up the typical ways in which we communicate as well. While speech itself is generally not a habit, the ways in which we use and convey it can be. These uses often entail corporeal components. As an act, speech has performative aspects that play out through our gestures, stances, and dispositional ways of speaking. Stephen, the captain of the jocks, may tend to stand authoritatively as he selects teammates on the football field, and April, a domineering white child, grabs children she is chiding and leans closely in toward their faces.[12] These bodily positionings are often done unknowingly and tend to convey messages, relations of power, emotional states, and the like to the witnesses of one's speech. Our patterns of word choice, as well as the tones and cadences we use to utter them, can also be habitual. For example, we may be prone to using certain words to describe our experiences or may employ certain slang when in a playground rather than classroom setting.

While they may vary from one person to the next, many people's habits are alike because they come about through similar transactions with the common world or are directed toward mutual objects in the environment. Moreover, because people experience many of the same things, they tend to develop similar habits. Because they are shared, those habits become customs. These are typical ways of acting that pervade a society. Often these customs bear normative judgment because they come to represent standards of good living within specific communities. Those customs then reinforce the development of similar habits in other people.[13]

Custom relies on the repetition of habit. Customs are based on the expectation that people will continue to perform the same acts and in the same ways. Assumptions about the similarity of habits across and between individuals and cultures, though, should be kept in check. Feminist pragmatist philosopher Shannon Sullivan correctly warns that "one cannot assume that bodily habits, behaviors, and structures automatically provide a common ground for communication and community that has not yet been inscribed by differences and particularities."[14] Even though members of the same community tend to transact with similar surroundings and thereby develop similar ways of behaving or thinking, the world is experienced slightly differently by each person, leading to the development of distinctive particularities in each. These differences allow for uniqueness of the self. Hence, similarity should not be assumed, especially as a starting point for communication. Failure to recognize differences can underlie misguided assumptions of commonality that inhibit successful transactions and communication.

Habits, Thought, and Will

The compulsive urge to act relates to desire. Habits give rise to desire and organize the body and environment in ways that allow desires to be pursued. The pursuit of desire is possible because habits carry out judgment and thought. Habits "do all the perceiving, recognizing, imagining, recalling, judging, conceiving and reasoning that is done."[15] This is to say not that reasoning, for example, *is* a habit but rather that habits provide the mechanisms that enable or enhance reasoning as well as carry out the activities that might result from reasoning.[16] Habits are the avenue through which the world is processed. The conditions sensed and experienced do not enter the body–mind straightforwardly. Habits filter and organize our perceptions, determining what environmental objects are noted and in what way. Habits, then, shape and precede our ideas. Ideas, or "thoughts of ends,"[17] as Dewey refers to them, are not created ex nihilo. Rather, our past bodily experience and habitual ways in which we have interacted with the world help us make sense of our experiences and to formulate these experiences in the shape of ideas. Without embodied understanding of ideas or their implications, ideas are meaningless.

Consider the case of race and gender. We habitually enact these identities (through the way we speak, move, and live) before we have a coherent idea of what it means to be a specific race or gender or before we are able to assign sophisticated meaning to these activities. Race and gender are historical products that precede us as individuals, yet we give rise to race and gender again and again by reproducing historical meanings through our habitual expression of them. It is habits that give us the felt, lived experience of being raced and gendered and that then enable us to ponder the significance of such living.

Finally, because habits are so closely tied to the environment via transaction, they do not think about or know the environment from a distant, reflective perspective. Indeed, habit itself cannot be said to think about or know certain propositions; rather, it takes the environment in and works with it, developing *know-how*—knowledge of how to act in the world. Habits provide "working capacities" that enable the enactment of thoughts and desires, while the habits themselves typically entail little or no thinking at all.[18]

The relationship between habit and thought is complex and continuous. Habit is necessary for the formation and enactment of thought; it is the means by which thought is able to transact with the material world. Or, in Dewey's words, "habits deprived of thought and thought which is futile are two sides of the same fact."[19] Some may wrongly proclaim that thought is the fount of intelligence and good living, while bodily habit inhibits one from making progress. Dewey aptly warns against this:

> To laud habit as conservative while praising thought as the main spring of progress is to take the surest course to making thought abstruse and irrelevant and progress a matter of accident and catastrophe. The concrete fact behind the current separation of body and mind, practice and theory, actualities and ideals, is precisely this separation of habit and thought. Thought which does not exist within ordinary habits of action lacks means of execution. In lacking application, it also lacks test, criterion.[20]

Habit, then, provides the means for implementing thoughts, intentions, and desires. Moreover, habit also allows those ideas to play out in the world in ways that test their accuracy or effectiveness and, hence, allows them to be improved or reworked. The reciprocal relationship between habit and thought continues when reflective thought leads to the formation of new, more fruitful and efficient habits. The ability of each person to engage in such reflection is dependent, however, on their individual skill, the guidance of others, and the power relationships in which they are embedded. This reflective element is particularly important to the role of schooling insofar as schools develop and oversee such skills and contain complex webs of power between students of various backgrounds. The unique position of schools is described in greater detail later.

Habits are active and projective. They constitute our ability to physically and mentally will ourselves. Dewey clarifies,

> We may think of habits as means, waiting, like tools in a box, to be used by conscious resolve. But they are something more than that. They are active means, means that project themselves, energetic and dominating ways of acting.[21]

Habits are always operating, each coming to the forefront of our activity individually or alongside other habits from one situation to the next. We do not encounter a stimulus and then begin acting; rather, we are always already acting. A stimulus is a change in the environment that relates to a change in our behavior, thereby bringing certain habits to the fore. Even when not at the forefront, our habits operate in covert ways, often provoking activity that entails their overt expression. When habits are repressed or denied expression, they often formulate ideas. Dewey provides the example of eating, a habit that, when unable to be fulfilled, constructs the sensation of hunger and the image of eating food. Even when not enacted, eating is an active habit, manifesting itself in the desire for food and bringing about changes in the environment that support its fulfillment.[22]

While it may be obvious that habits lead to bodily actions, like eating, it is becoming clear that, for Dewey, habits are often linked to intelligence. For even though habits tend to function at the level of the unconscious, this is not to say that they cannot be brought into conscious consideration. Steven Fesmire clarifies, "Pragmatism views habit not in terms of a condition *reflex*, but in terms of intelligent reconstruction of problematic situations."[23] When formed tentatively as hypotheses in light of intelligent foresight into future, unpredictable circumstances, habits can be flexible agents of change whose form emerges as situations unfold. Or, in Dewey's words, "the intellectual element in a habit fixes the relation of the habit to varied and elastic use, and hence to continued growth."[24] In this way, habits, as intimately tied to intelligent reflection, are projective and sites of agency. They can be changed in ways that change the subject and, through transaction, can effect change in the world as well. The heart of agency lies in the process of acquiring new habits and changing old ones, as I detail in chapter 5.

Even when revealed as problematic (perhaps because they are oppressive, unjust, or outdated), habits cannot be simply dropped. Because the subject is constituted and enabled by cultural structures and norms, we should not try to overthrow habits entirely (as though we could be freed from them) but rather rework them in liberating ways. Indeed, it is nonsensical to suppose the complete removal of habit. Instead, Dewey proposes the replacement of old habits by those that are more intelligent and just. Ideally, because habits are "adjustments *of* the environment, not merely *to* it," adopting new habits (through a careful process of intellectual reflection of by other means) can change the environmental phenomena that produced the problematic old habit.[25]

Intriguingly, given the common understanding of habit as ongoing repetition of specific acts, Dewey argues that habits must not necessarily be repeated. He claims, "Repetition is in no sense the essence of habit. Tendency to repeat acts is an incident of many habits but not of all."[26] It is possible, though rare, for a person to develop a predilection that never comes to pass again because the environmental conditions which first formed the habit never reoccur. Given transaction, repetition happens after a habit is formed if the environment stays the same and the continued action proves useful, although in the cases of bad habits, repetition may continue regardless of changing environments and uselessness of a habit. Most habits are and, in many cases, must be repeated, especially those that culturally position the subject and are necessary for continued recognition. Many habits require exercising in order for them to continue to function with ease and therefore are repeated. Because of this, I believe repetition is generally an appropriate criterion for assessing whether an activity is a habit, though Dewey would hold out the exception noted here. The likelihood of repetition allows us to differentiate habitual activities from other type of activities, like a sneeze, because they are standing predilections.

Dewey contends that organisms are bound to repeat but not particular things or reflections of a stagnant world:

> The essence of habit is an acquired predisposition to *ways* or modes of response, not to particular acts except as, under special conditions, these express a way of behaving. Habit means special sensitivities or accessibility to certain classes of stimuli, standing predilections and aversions, rather than bare recurrence of specific acts.[27]

Habits show a proclivity; what and how they repeat may vary. These variations on repetition are often provoked by change in the environment or unsatisfactory states. Because repetition may vary, a space is opened up for newness—a space for growth and a space for learning. Moreover, within that space, new variations and new habits can be tried out. Their quality can be assessed using pragmatist principles of growth and flourishing. Good habits, then, are not simply those that continually change but those that fruitfully lead from one satisfactory experience to the next and do so in ways that are ethical and improve the conditions for living. Good habits promote smooth and just transactions with other people and the world at large.

Bad Habits

While habit provides a platform for transaction with the world and implements thought, habits can become problematic. When habits fail to keep up with a changing world, they become stagnant and routine; we become "stuck in a bad habit." According to Dewey, "what makes a habit bad is enslavement to old ruts."[28] We become stuck in a rut when we continue to behave in a certain way again and again even though that behavior is not working for us, insofar as it inhibits our growth, blocks fruitful exchanges with others, or does not help us navigate the world.

When we fall prey to the comfort and ease of repeating habits that once served us well, even habits that were once good may become bad. Because the world is constantly changing, even those good habits must change, for they may no longer serve to coordinate action in the evolving world. Our satisfaction with simply getting by may prevent us from seeing that the world has changed, demanding new activity on our part. We may become careless or even oblivious to the world around us.[29] For example, a boy may discover that shouting out correct answers during the first week of class earns the admiration of his peers and attracts the attention of the teacher. While this may initially be a good habit, it becomes bad once the dynamics of the class have changed and the boy has not. His classmates may grow frustrated, for example, that their patiently raised hands are not called on because the boy beats them to the punch, or the teacher may begin to lose interest in his exuberant outbursts. The boy may be so stuck in this habit that he will continue it even if he sees it as no longer fruitful. Habits can become deeply engrained and very difficult to change.

For Dewey,

> A bad habit suggests an inherent tendency to action and also a hold, command over us. It makes us do things we are ashamed of, things which we tell ourselves we prefer not to do. It overrides our formal resolutions, our conscious decisions. When we are honest with ourselves we acknowledge that a habit has this power because it is so intimately a part of ourselves. It has a hold upon us because we are the habit.[30]

Even though these bad habits appear overwhelming when described as such, we are generally not conscious of them, and they have no meaning for us because they are not connected to ends. Because we do not reflect on them, meaning is unable to arise from consideration of their consequences, shortcomings, and successes. Hence, they fail to be educative and to guide our lives in fruitful ways.

Habits can become compartmentalized in ways that shield them from the interpenetration of other habits, from being reconsidered given their confliction with other habits, or from keeping up with the changing world. When this happens, habits maintain a static, routine specialization that is often perceived by others as narrow-mindedness or lack of depth, self-knowledge, or complexity in a person.[31]

Bad habits are those that prevent smooth, ethical, or successful interaction between people. Such social exchanges may be inhibited because of a bodily habit that sets up or maintains boundaries between people, blocking communication or activities that would improve the well-being of each person. Debra Van Ausdale and Joe Feagin share an interesting example of a preschooler's disturbing behavior:

> Carla, a three-year-old child, is preparing herself for resting time. She picks up her cot and starts to move it to the other side of the classroom. A teacher asks what she is doing. "I need to move this," explains Carla. "Why?" asks the teacher. "Because I can't sleep next to a nigger," Carla says, pointing to Nicole, a four-year-old Black child on a cot nearby. "Niggers are stinky. I can't sleep next to one." Stunned, the teacher, who is white, tells Carla to move her cot back and not to use "hurting words." Carla looks amused but complies.[32]

While it may appear that Carla simply holds a false, racist belief that black people smell badly, I propose that her actions could better be understood as bad habits. Over time, her inclination to avoid black people and maintain a separate physical space has congealed into a habit. In this classroom, when the environmental conditions arose that placed her nearby a black child, she was led by habit to move her cot. She does so casually, as though her activity were perfectly normal and justified. When probed for an explanation for her actions, she is forced to consider her rationale, but she does so lightheartedly in a way that protects her habit from genuine scrutiny and prevents her from seeing that her actions are preventing her from getting to know the black girl and are perpetuating racially segregated spaces. Her habit, then, is rigid and unintelligent, preventing fruitful interaction between herself and others.

Carla's habit may also be classified as bad because it is harmful. The words she is prone to using and the racial spaces she carves out may harm Nicole, other black people, or even Carla herself. Of course, we often understand the infamous bad habit of smoking in terms of this sense of harm to oneself and others. We also understand smoking and other habits like it to be bad because they are addictive. They carry a compulsiveness that is very hard to overcome, even when the harmful effects of the habit are consciously known to the person.

BOURDIEU'S HABITUS

In the past decade, sociologist Pierre Bourdieu earned both credit and criticism for his effort to explain human behavior and social reproduction through his concept of the habitus. He defines the habitus as "structured, structuring dispositions" in his work *The Logic of Practice*.[33] A redundant-sounding definition, the double sense of structure that he invokes describes the habitus as both dispositions that are effected, or formed by, environmental conditions and then, in turn, also affect their surroundings. This relationship sounds quite similar to the Deweyan-inspired transactive encounter I draw on where habits both arise from and participate in the exchange between environment and organism. The dispositions are structured by these transactions with the cultural world, yet they impact and shape their surroundings as well.

For Bourdieu, our environment conditions us and produces dispositions and structures for understanding and organizing our experiences in the world. We use these dispositions, the habitus, to know our world and to guide our actions in it. Much like Deweyan habits, the habitus enables us to form hypotheses about the future and to fashion our behavior accordingly. Importantly, however, the habitus is unreflective and subconscious. It guides our interpretations of the world and our actions without our conscious reflection. It cannot be actively called into consideration in the same way that many Deweyan habits can and, in some cases, should be.

Unlike Deweyan habits that are seated primarily in current situations and transactional events, Bourdieu says that "the anticipations of the habitus, practical hypotheses based on past experience, give disproportionate weight to early experiences."[34] These early experiences overwhelmingly shape the way present situations are understood and acted on. Contemporary contextual nuances have far less sway over the activities of the habitus than Deweyan habits.

The habitus influences perception, but it gears perception and action toward socially acceptable beliefs and behaviors:

> The habitus, a product of history, produces individual and collective practices—
> more history—in accordance with the schemes generated by history. It ensures
> the active presence of past experiences, which deposited in each organism in the
> form of schemes of perception, thought and action, then guarantee the "correct-
> ness" of practices and their constancy over time, more reliably than all formal
> rules and explicit norms.[35]

Early experiences, including schooling for Bourdieu, and the internalization of culturally acceptable behavior over time normatively shape and nearly determine our behaviors. Habitus, then, internalizes environmental conditions, including cultural norms, making them appear natural. It reifies the social field, making it appear real and, in some cases, fixed. In this way, habitus behaves like the sedimentation of gender performatives Butler describes. It bears a long history of incorporating cultural norms in ways that make the performances of these norms and certain aspects of the bodies that enact them appear naturally fixed.

Habitus leads to thoughts that appear to be free and unrestricted but are actually bounded by the previous experiences and existing structures that initially gave rise to the habitus. In result, the beliefs and activities of members of a society are well coordinated. Bourdieu initially says that is because they are guided by shared habitus that develops from "identical histories."[36] As I described earlier in terms of Deweyan habits, however, I would reply that even though environmental conditions may be similar, no two people experience them in precisely the same way. Because of this, habits, while showing similarity in many cases, do vary from one person to the next. Later in his writing, Bourdieu concedes much the same point but still holds that across a social class, members are likely to have a shared habitus because "the conditionings associated with a particular class of conditions of existence produce habitus."[37]

Bourdieu's conceptual framework may lend some insight to the development of habits and may bring Dewey's notion into more recent philosophical and sociological discussions. Nonetheless, while the habitus may show some similarity to habits as I portray them here, I caution the reader against seeing them interchangeably, for doing so would severely misrepresent the unique notion of habit I develop in the coming chapters.

CONCLUSION

In sum, "habit," as it is used in this book, differs considerably from its definition in everyday parlance:

> The word habit may seem twisted somewhat from its customary use when employed as we have been using it. But we need a word to express that kind of human activity which is influenced by prior activity and is in that sense acquired; which contains within itself a certain ordering or systematization of minor elements of action; which is projective, dynamic in quality, ready for overt manifestation; and which is operative in some subdued subordinate form even when not obviously dominating activity.[38]

Indeed, habits should not be thought of in the simplistic sense of addictive repetition invoked by contemporary use of the term. Rather, habits are far more complex and comprehensive. They entail both what the person is and what the person does. In Dewey's words, they "constitute the self."[39] This includes, as I argue in the next two chapters, the raced and gendered self.

While certainly not an exhaustive list of the different types of habit, I have included some of the habits most central to understanding identity—and race and gender in particular—at the end of this chapter. I have provided brief descriptions of these types of habits as well as examples. These types of habits vary in the ways in which they are classified as habits, but, excluding the last two, nearly all fulfill most of the Deweyan criteria described in this chapter:

- Demands for activity; they lead us to do something
- Allow us to operate with ease
- Performed without belabored effort
- Proclivities to act in certain ways
- Often filter, organize, and enact perceptions and thoughts
- Almost always repeated

The next chapter explains, via a historical analysis of biological and anthropological science, how race is constituted and classified by and through habits. Understanding race through the nuanced lens of a Deweyan account of habit will open new avenues for interpreting the history of race and envisioning its future as well as for making sense of racism and envisioning its end.

Table 2.1.   Types of Habit

Type of Habit	Descriptive Features	Examples
Comportment	Gestures, movements, ways of carrying one's body	Swagger, standing with authority
Skills	Almost always have mental components, know-how, produces a product	Driving, typing, singing
Habits of mind	Intellectual virtues, ways of thinking	Hasty judgment, careful deliberation, patient consideration of consequences
Dispositions	Personality traits, general demeanor	The tomboy Annette's defiance, curiosity
Habits of conduct	Practical knowledge of socially acceptable actions, often guided by morals	Engaging in standard salutations, being kind
Ways of communicating	Patterns of language choice, presentation of the body when speaking, tone, speed	A tendency to shout when frustrated, using slang around friends
Appearance	Typical ways of dressing or styling one's hair and makeup, hygiene practices	Wearing fancy clothes on Sundays, girls wearing ponytails when playing sports
Ways of perceiving	Sensitivities, attractions to certain aspects of objects	Noticing variations in skin color, noting a trait like hair texture but not another
Bad habits	Compulsive addictions that control us, don't meet changes or demands of the environment, harmful	Smoking, aggression
Habitus	Structured dispositions formed out of past experiences, produce shared social practices, unconscious	Learning one's mother tongue, ways of working, lifestyle of the working class

NOTES

1. See John Dewey, *Experience and Nature* (Chicago: Open Court, 1925), 217 and elsewhere.

2. Dewey, *Experience and Nature*, 66. For more on this verbalizing, see Shannon Sullivan, *Living across and through Skins: Transactional Bodies, Pragmatism, and Feminism* (Bloomington: University of Indiana Press, 2001), and Bruce Wilshire, "Body-Mind and Subconsciousness: Tragedy in Dewey's Life and Work," in *Philosophy and the Reconstruction of Culture: Pragmatic Essays after Dewey*, ed. John J. Stuhr (Albany: State University of New York Press, 1993), 264.

3. John Dewey, *Human Nature and Conduct* (1922; reprint, Mineola, N.Y.: Dover, 2002), 154.

4. This occurs particularly within his discussion of existence versus essence, where the former are the metaphysically given. For more, see Jim Garrison, "What a Long Strange Trip It's Been, or, The Metaphysics of Presence: Derrida and Dewey on Human Development," in *Philosophy of Education Society Yearbook*, ed. Lynda Stone (Urbana: University of Illinois Press, 2000), 4.

5. Gert J. J. Biesta and Nicholas C. Burbules, *Pragmatism and Educational Research* (Lanham, Md.: Rowman & Littlefield, 2003), 26.

6. Donna Haraway, "A Cyborg Manifesto: Science, Technology, and Socialist-Feminism in the Late Twentieth Century," in *Simians, Cyborgs, and Women: The Reinvention of Nature* (New York: Routledge, 1991), quoted in Judith Butler, *Bodies That Matter: On the Discursive Limits of "Sex"* (New York: Routledge, 1993), 1.

7. Dewey, *Human Nature and Conduct*, 90.

8. Dewey, *Human Nature and Conduct*, 141.

9. Megan Boler further discusses this in *Feeling Power: Emotions and Education* (New York: Routledge, 1999), 193.

10. Dewey, *Human Nature and Conduct*, 25.

11. Biesta and Burbules, *Pragmatism and Educational Research*, 38.

12. Paul Connolly, *Racism, Gender Identities, and Young Children* (London: Routledge, 1998), 110; Debra Van Ausdale and Joe R. Feagin, *The First R: How Children Learn Race and Racism* (Lanham, Md.: Rowman & Littlefield, 2001), 112. These are real children who are discussed in later examples.

13. Dewey, *Human Nature and Conduct*, 58.

14. Sullivan, *Living across and through Skins*, 74.

15. Dewey, *Human Nature and Conduct*, 177.

16. Dewey clarifies, "Yet habit does not, of itself, know, for it does not of itself stop to think, observe or remember. . . . Habit incorporates, enacts or overrides objects, but it doesn't know them. Impulse scatters and obliterates them with its restless stir. A certain delicate combination of habit and impulse is requisite for observation, memory and judgment. Knowledge which is not projected against the black unknown lives in the muscles, not in consciousness." *Human Nature and Conduct*, 177.

17. Dewey, *Human Nature and Conduct*, 30.

18. Dewey, *Human Nature and Conduct*, 177, 25.

19. Dewey, *Human Nature and Conduct*, 67.

20. Dewey, *Human Nature and Conduct*, 67.

21. Dewey, *Human Nature and Conduct*, 25.

22. Dewey, *Human Nature and Conduct*, 53.

23. Steven A. Fesmire, "Educating the Moral Artist: Dramatic Rehearsal in Moral Education," *Studies in Philosophy and Education* 13, no. 3–4 (1994–95): 216.

24. Dewey, *Democracy and Education*, 48.

25. Dewey, *Human Nature and Conduct*, 52.

26. Dewey, *Human Nature and Conduct*, 42.

27. Dewey, *Human Nature and Conduct*, 42.

28. Dewey, *Human Nature and Conduct*, 66.

29. I grant that such an experience could be only temporary, for the dissonance with the environment that would be produced would almost certainly eventually cast the faulty habit into doubt, according to Dewey.

30. Dewey, *Human Nature and Conduct*, 24.

31. Dewey, *Human Nature and Conduct*, 38–39.

32. Van Ausdale and Feagin, *The First R*, 1.

33. Bourdieu, *Logic of Practice*, 52.

34. Bourdieu, *Logic of Practice*, 54.

35. Bourdieu, *Logic of Practice*, 54.

36. Bourdieu, *Logic of Practice*, 59.

37. Bourdieu, *Logic of Practice*, 53; see also 59.

38. Dewey, *Human Nature and Conduct*, 40–41.

39. Dewey, *Human Nature and Conduct*, 25.

Chapter Three

A Historical Look at the Making of Race

From physical education classes to chemistry labs, students learn to identify and sort groups from an early age. Often, racial differences play a role in group selection. An elementary art project reveals an interesting example. The students were tasked with creating a banner displaying their names and handprints. The children were given an array of paints to use for the project. In order to decide who should use which paints to color their handprints, the children looked for colors that best matched their skin. All the white children easily selected the same shade of peach paint. Corinne, an African/white biracial girl, broke protocol by selecting a dark brown paint for one handprint and a light brown paint for the other. Three black children drew attention from their white peers, however, when they selected a pink paint to represent their handprints. Against the admonishment of an outspoken white child, April, who claimed that pink only rightfully matched white children, Taleshia (black) explained that the pink matched her rosy palms. Two other black kids chose to depict one handprint in pink and one in dark brown.[1] These decisions created quite a stir among several students who were torn over how to appropriately assign color, determine which parts of the body most significantly portrayed color, and whether one's artistic display of self should be racially confined.

Scientists are also often concerned with racial identification and classification. These activities have taken interesting form as scientists have struggled to understand racial classification. A conception of race held by many early modern Western scientists (and still today by some people) was that races are immutable and determined human differences. Often, external physical variations were thought to be indicative of innate, fixed differences. Race was— and frequently still is—a classification system based on physical characteristics of the body that can be used to describe and make predictions about human groups. Advances in biology and anthropology over the past few decades have produced evidence that this view is not valid. Drawing on genetic analyses and intricate study of cultural variations, many of these contemporary scientists proclaim that race is not a legitimate classificatory scheme because human variations do not map onto race as a biological concept with a one-to-one correspondence. Agreeing, theorists of social construction from the biological and social sciences as well as the humanities have explained that race *in itself* is nonexistent; rather, it is a product of social practices, language systems, aesthetic values, and divisive behaviors.

Race is a historical product that, despite the efforts of some social constructionists and scientists to herald its end, is continually being reproduced in the way it is popularly invoked, enacted, used as a label, and responded to. While some social constructionists recently have conceded that race continues to function as reality in everyday life (e.g., Audrey Smedley), few (and even fewer biologists) have accounted for the extent to which people experience themselves and their lives as raced in ways that surpass a biological understanding of categorization. Often people proclaim a deep affinity with their racial identity, arguing that the way they and others perceive their bodies and actions or the ways in which they coalesce with some groups and not others prove that they belong to a specific racial category. I suggest that the mismatch between the proclamations of these scientists and those of common people is due to an underlying phenomena that science unknowingly adopted, developed, reified, and in some ways continues to perpetuate—racialized habits.

Although the scientific history of studying basic physical features, like skin color and bodily dimensions, among races has been well documented, few historians of science have overtly considered how race has been constructed, signified, and studied via corporeal habit. Many historians have studied race in terms of how the body *appears*, but few have studied race in terms of what the body *does*.[2] These habits constitute how the body is in the world—the default and seemingly natural ways in which it acts, moves, and communicates. Formed through transactions between the environment and biological makeup, these habits shape the way our body both appears and operates. While it is not a contradiction for social constructionists to hold that race is both artificially produced and socially real, few have considered how scientific, social, and discursive matrices materialize into bodily racial habits.

As I described in the previous chapter, habits are the organization and meaning of one's bodily impulses that are formed through one's transaction with the world. They are also embodied beliefs that one obtains through inquiry into one's surroundings. The impulses and beliefs assemble into patterns or styles of being in the world that one performs effortlessly and largely without conscious reflection. They can be recognized as skills, attitudes, ways of communicating, sensitivities, modes of response, gestures, dispositions, or bodily comportments. While they may vary from one person to the next, some habits or elements of habits are shared because they come about through similar transactions with the common world or are directed toward mutual objects in the environment. When reflected on, analyzed, and categorized, these habits acquire meaning, including racial definition. Moreover, the habits reproduce the historical meanings of race.

In this chapter, I trace the study of racial habits from early modern science through contemporary genetic biology. I offer a genealogy of race in the sense defined by Michel Foucault and Butler where "genealogy investigates the political stakes in designating as an *origin* and *cause* those identity categories that are in fact the *effects* of institutions, practices, discourses with multiple and diffuse points of origin."[3] I show how the interests of traders, farmers, and scientists were served, in turn, by defining race as an innate category that plays out in habits. Notably, those served were almost always whites; a drastically disproportionate amount of effort was spent analyzing the habits of minorities, presumably to establish their inferiority. Moreover, I suggest that the classification of race in terms of habit is a product of science and of habitual ways of perceiving other people. It is the result of drawing attention and meticulous scientific analysis to certain bodily aspects and not others when comparing human groups and thereby of unjustifiably assigning meaning (often bearing hierarchical or normative significance) to some traits and not others. Finally, carrying an emphasis on transaction into this historical analysis reveals how the meaning of race has changed as the habits of scientists and their subjects have changed over time.

These historical ways of observing and categorizing others continue to impact the way contemporary people view themselves and others, including students within schools and the social policies that organize them. One British researcher relates a telling instance. At an urban English primary school, there is considerable animosity toward the South Asian boys from the white and black boys. Often on the playground, the white and black boys dominated the central public spaces, while South Asian boys avoid confrontation by hiding in the bushes bordering the playground. The black and white boys were asked if they would allow a South Asian boy to play with them. They say only one, Prajay, can play because he does not wear a dot on his forehead, is not small, and is not a slow runner—characteristics that they perceive in other South Asian boys and that echo the descriptions their teachers give of South Asian boys as effeminate, small, defenseless, and eager to please. Even Prajay is constantly at risk for verbal and physical attack when playing and is pushed to the ground and called a "Paki." Rather than playing football, most of the South Asian boys create fantasy games where they role-play monsters, superheroes, and cartoon characters. The teachers described these boys and their games as "silly" and "immature."[4] The boys also, however, engaged in more stereotypical and age-appropriate masculine activities like kickboxing and racing each other and teased one another about prospective love interests. These activities went largely unnoticed by other students and teachers.[5] Indeed, we see in this example that teachers and white students categorize South Asian students by their slowness, delicateness, quietness, and eagerness to please. They designate racial distinction by assigning significance to some habits and not others. Moreover, they overlook variations of similar habits that both whites and South Asians share, like running on the football field (whites) or racing each other on the sidelines (South Asians), in order to maintain beliefs in distinctly separated groups. This suggests that habits of race can be read in multiple ways in varying contexts and can depend on the viewpoint, beliefs, race, and other characteristics of the observer as well.

HABITS AND THE HISTORY OF RACE IN SCIENCE

At least as early as the ancient Egyptians and Greeks, groups of people began to distinguish themselves from one another according to physical appearance, occupation, language, and ways of living. Or, in the words of the Egyptian hieroglyphic poem, "The Great Hymn to Aten,"

> Their tongues are separate in speech,
> And their natures as well;
> Their skins are distinguished,
> As thou distinguishest the foreign peoples.[6]

Adopting similar criteria, the Greeks distinguished themselves from the barbarians in terms of speech (the Greeks believed the barbarians could only utter "bar, bar, bar"), brutish behavior, and comportment. The objects and criteria of classification, then, pre-dated modern or even premodern, science. The concept of race and its applicability grew out of everyday language. And, as Robert Kuttner remarks, it is best to understand the term "race" by examining the objects to which scientists have applied it.[7] Moreover, it is fruitful to examine the conceptual exchange between science and common folk, including the ways in which nonscientists legitimated racial distinction as significant and then, buying into its importance, scientists taught the public how to perceive, determine, and interpret race. Of note, both influenced each other's decisions regarding which habits were significant for determining racial distinction, thereby leading race to be defined in certain ways and rendering bodies that were ambivalent in their display of those specific habits marginalized or not materialized enough to matter for science.

Moving historically closer to the advent of modern science, Smedley traces the rise of racial distinction, hierarchy, and slavery in her seminal work, *Race in North America: Origin and Evolution of a Worldview*.[8] Smedley describes the fear and tension that escalated between the English and Irish during the sixteenth and seventeenth centuries. She locates this as a key historical moment in the development of notions of racial difference. Important for my work here, this difference was predicated on habits that distinguished groups. For, in this case, the English characterized the Irish by their habits of conduct and communication: their brutish social skills, immoral lawlessness, and uncivilized manner of speech. Their differences were noted not simply at the level of physical features but more so by the ways in which they characteristically acted. The English normatively labeled their own habits as superior to those displayed by the Irish and feared that degeneracy among their people might result because of immigration or interbreeding.

The English developed the image of the savage to encapsulate the habits, values, and laws of the Irish. This set the precedent for how the English treated other groups of people they encountered during trade and exploration. When the English were introduced to Africans, the Irish-like heathen ways of living they perceived among this population led them to label the Africans "savages" as well. It was only later, as the savage description began to justify enslavement, that the dark skin and basic physical features of the Africans came to symbolize the image specified in the name "savage."[9] This shift set the course for future conflation between race as simple physical difference and more complex habitual differences in ways of living that impacted bodily form.

While French physician Francois Bernier was the first scientist to classify races by skin color in 1684, others continued to distinguish groups in much more complex ways.[10] A century later, American whites began to differentiate among black-skinned people according to their habits of conduct, skills, and dispositions. Ira Berlin has charted the categorical distinctions that Chesapeake planters created to demarcate Africans from Creoles. These whites noted differences in habit, including working motivation and skill as well as proficiency at white-sounding English.[11] Thereby, these populations who, by base physical characteristics, were the same became distinguished. And the Creoles, whose habits were commended over those of the Africans (often because they more closely resembled those of the planters themselves), were rewarded with better treatment. The planters later came to see, however, that the Africans could adopt Creole ways, in effect becoming Creole and closer to whites. Hence, they recognized, though perhaps not at the level of explicit consciousness, that bodily habits did not correspond to distinct innate categories and could be shaped. These farmers realized that setting up a graduated distinction within a subordinate racial group jeopardized the completeness of their dominance, and therefore they curtailed the practice.

Perhaps sensing the pressing need within public domains to identify racial characteristics that could genuinely distinguish different races (because of the need of whites to secure and maintain superiority within the political and economic realms), Johann Blumenbach, George-Louis Leclerc de Buffon, and other leading scientists working in the mid- to late 1700s sought to definitively determine which characteristics denoted racial separation. And it was naturalist Carolus Linnaeus whose 1735 *Natural System* first pinned down an extensive system of racial difference.[12] While they were drawn to many of the traits that contemporary commoners may name as racial markers, like skin color and facial features, they understood these markers to arise not simply from the way the body looks but also from the way the body acts. For example, they posited that skin color arose from climate, social class, or profession—hence, from the location and styles in which the body typically positions itself.[13]

Their hypothesis on the formation of African flat noses and large lips is even more noteworthy for understanding how bodily habits of comportment have become conflated with physical features that correspond to fixed innate races. They suggested that these facial features resulted from the ways in which African mothers routinely carried their babies pressed against their backs in pouches while working, thereby flattening the noses of their babies. Employing an early Lamarkian notion, they argued that these traits then became fixed over time and were inherited without the actual physical manipulation necessarily occurring to each baby. Head shape of children was also speculated to depend on the customary way mothers laid their babies down to sleep (on their backs or sides) or by the way in which midwives handled newborns. Finally, Ethiopian flared noses were thought to arise from the heavy breathing of pregnant women performing lower-class, manual labor.[14] Thus, the physical trait of the nose was thought to be a result of the way the body adapted to its strenuous environment and developed habitual ways of coping with it.

In 1787, reverend and scientist Samuel Stanhope Smith noted similar effects of social class and type of work on the physical appearance and comportment of slaves who worked in the house rather than the field and vice versa. He was led to claim that "social factors even influenced bodily conformation and facial lineaments."[15] Hence, the body was shaped by interaction with the environment, and this shaping took on varying significance relative to the type of activity performed. Here, Smith calls to mind the permeability of the body via transaction described in the Deweyan account of habits in chapter 2. Each of these examples shows how racial distinction, including bodily appearance, was understood as relative to the habitual ways in which certain people behaved and carried their bodies or those of their children. These methods of distinction gave rise to coherent systems of classification, including Blumenbach's pyramid model, that both vindicated and clarified the popular views of the race-discerning general public, especially those of traders and travelers who encountered differently appearing people most often.

In the 1770s, scientific discourse on race began to overtly categorize racial differences as hierarchical. While Carolus Linnaeus, the Swedish father of taxonomy, described the habits of different groups but did not claim to rank them, he used descriptive language that evoked levels of superiority. He described "*H. europaeus* as active and acute, as a discoverer; and *H. afer* as crafty, lazy, and careless."[16] It was in 1774 when Edward Long, much like the English of the preceding century, described African habits in terms of degeneracy that the linking of early scientific understandings of race with authoritative and hierarchical models became more explicit.[17] These descriptive, normative terms were picked up by people of all sorts, including those as prominent as Thomas Jefferson. In 1786 and for many years to come, Jefferson depicted race in terms of moral sense, intelligence, aesthetics, bravery, color, and odor.[18] Examining patterns in the comportment of blacks, these criteria led him to later conclude that African inferiority is evident in their moral and mental characteristics.[19] Hierarchical descriptions of racial difference likely often moved in the other direction as well; the general public may have used these words in their daily lives and turned to science to validate them as justification for slavery, racism, and other systems of oppression and preference.

Writing at about the same time, Lord Karnes extended the scientific analysis of these racial markers in terms of their internal counterparts and significance. He declared that internal differences of character and temperament were more important than external differences and are based in fixed innate sources.[20] It was these internal and fixed traits that played out in corporeal habit that worried early nineteenth-century American government officials when it came to biracial white/Native American babies. It was not that they worried about how the babies looked in terms of color, cheekbone shape, or other surface level features but rather what habits of conduct and mind they displayed. The officials were curious to see if the babies would exhibit "white ways" and therefore could be used to potentially civilize the Indian tribes where they often lived.[21]

As the nineteenth century progressed, biracial offspring became a growing concern in America and elsewhere. Children who did not fit easily into one racial category or another incited fear and concern among scientists and the public. In part, these feelings may have resulted because these children challenged the standard way of perceiving the world's inhabitants—as fitting neatly into discrete racial categories. Scientists responded by developing more complex analyses of racial makeup, including shifting the object of analysis internally, where it was believed that one's race could definitively be determined. In classrooms today, we continue to see students who seek an internal certainty for race, even if only at very basic levels. Van Ausdale and Feagin, for example, describe one young black boy who tries to identify other students by their colors but is particularly perplexed by one white-appearing girl. He tries to cut the girl to definitively determine her race, later explaining to the teacher, "I wanted to see what she looked like underneath."[22]

The effort to establish internal analysis ushered in not only phrenology and craniometry but also logical positivism. This paradigm upheld race as a real and measurable phenomenon. Scientists interested in internal traits and psychometricians interested in intelligence believed racial habits and behaviors could be defined and measured "absolutely or operationally."[23] Once measured, the habitual quality was reified as reflecting an innate, fixed property of an individual. The habit was thereby stripped of social context, leaving the trait to be seen as the property of an individual rather than arising out of a situation that demands or cultivates intelligence, speed, and so on. Hence, "processes of interaction" became reified.[24] This fixation of a property within the individual provided a platform for twentieth-century scientists to argue that intelligence and other internal traits may vary across a continuum of individuals who fall into racially hierarchical groups.

Crainiometrists of the 1820s and 1830s, like Samuel Morton, matched intellectual achievement, levels of activity, and moods of races to crania measurements.[25] Phrenologists of the 1830s matched traits such as thievery, destructiveness, sensuality, cunningness, cruelty, and pride to parts of the brain and skull and to their dimensions.[26] With the advent of phrenology, scientists began to enact the reification within individuals and groups just described. They moved from an analysis of individuals and their variations to categorizing those variations as types, that is, races.

A few decades later, interested in many of the moral traits analyzed by the phrenologists, Sir Francis Galton argued that the weakness of human nature is displayed in dispositions and human habits of conduct.[27] These bodily weaknesses prevent humans from living to the fullest guidelines of morality. According to Galton, observers identify some races as savage by virtue of their bodily displayed habits, including faulty moral dispositions, even though those people observed may actually be aware of and be working toward morality. For Galton, then, habits became not only a marker of racial differences but also a marker of morality, thereby fostering a normative link between gradations of races and moral uprightness. One statistician in particular, Frederick Hoffman, spent extensive time cataloging the "tendencies" and "traits" of blacks, including proclivities to immorality and criminality.[28] Specific body parts of blacks were also investigated because they were thought to symbolize morality. This was the case with the extensive measurements performed on Hottentot female buttocks and genitals because they were thought to signify immoral sexuality.[29] As David Roediger documented in his discussion of whites as working class from 1800 to 1860, whites perpetuated this normative racial hierarchy of morality, conferring the image of the preindustrial wild savage onto the bodies of blacks and engaging in immoral escapades themselves when painted in blackface.[30]

Galton believed that immoral habits and bodily comportments were inheritable, leading him to father "eugenics."[31] Galton wanted the more intelligent and morally upright (whites) to have more children than those who were not, thereby rightfully populating and directing the future world.[32] When phenotypic traits started to blur in North America and Europe in the late nineteenth century, due in part to immigration and interbreeding, the notion of "racial essence" came about. It stressed particular temperaments, intelligence levels, and morality that were inherited as a racial bunch despite changing physical appearance.[33] Galton's work, especially his declaration that every type of human faculty was heritable,[34] served to bolster this view. Over time, the beliefs of eugenicists trickled into school textbooks and popular rhetoric used in classrooms as Galton and his followers employed schools to institutionalize their racial hierarchies.

Mid-nineteenth-century attempts to define racial purity and degrees of intermediateness led scientists to investigate which traits were transmitted to new generations over time and to what degree. Such efforts largely served to keep the notion of race as discrete and "internally homogeneous."[35] Charles Darwin, writing slightly before and during the time of Galton, pursued the study of heredity, leading him to challenge the discreteness of race to an extent.

In *The Origin of Species*, Darwin studied how habitual traits of distinctly typed dogs were inherited and mingled through breeding and crossbreeding.[36] His observations of canines impacted his studies of humans, particularly his focus of analysis. Darwin studied the physical traits, emotional displays, intelligence, communication skills, and bodily tendencies of people of different races in much the same way that he studied those of dogs. He examined not only how their bodies appear on the surface but also how they acted most comfortably and most often. Not only were habits used by Darwin as his object of study, but the ability to adopt new habits and change old ones when exposed to new environments became a key criterion for Darwin in distinguishing "civilized" and "savage" races.[37] Darwin believed that habits of a man can first be learned voluntarily but later come so quickly that they appear as natural reflex.[38] Hence, habits come to be indistinguishable from what the man *is*. Darwin and Dewey show considerable similarity in their views of habit formation, the indistinguishability of the man from his habits, and, as we shall see in chapter 5, the importance of changing habits.

Following his observations of differently raced people, Darwin was led to acknowledge variations in terms of intellect, imagination, curiosity, and morals. Importantly, though, he claims that these are subtle graduations between races rather than distinct separations that can be classified as discrete types.[39] This declaration, relying on a more gradual continuum image of human variation, worked against the then popular notion of race as fixed and distinct separation.

The rise of psychology, paralleled by social Darwinism, at the end of the nineteenth and beginning of the twentieth centuries further directed racial analysis toward the internal and mental. Despite Darwin's proposed continuum, understanding of hierarchical habits as being capable of being cultivated within "inferior" races, and his own disgust at the effects of slavery on the bodily reflexes of blacks,[40] social Darwinists tried to apply principles of heredity and natural selection as grounds for race and race differences. They supported a racial "survival of the fittest." In this view, economic and social success were thought to be the just rewards for the most fit or evolved humans, those who were the smartest, most moral, and most aesthetically pleasing. In a strange twist of logic, the fact that whites had attained those levels of success was thought to demonstrate that whites must be the fittest race. When race (and racial hierarchy) is understood as natural, legal, medical, and scientific acts are thought to justifiably follow from it. Formal decisions to privilege certain groups become permissible. This was certainly the case during the reign of social Darwinism and, some would argue, continues today.

Large-scale intelligence testing beginning with and following World War I served to bolster the claims of psychologists and social Darwinists. One test in particular, the SAT, was devised in 1925 by racial separatist Carl Campbell Bingham to establish a merit-based criterion for keeping blacks out of college.[41] These tests showed whites to be superior in almost every aspect of intelligence. Their use as separators of social groups, assigning intelligence-appropriate tasks, careers, and educational opportunities, reified notions of fixed internal race by perpetuating certain races of people in specific types of work and social classes and preventing them from progressing over the next several decades. And while at the end of the nineteenth century both scientists and the public shared an integrated concept of race as embodying physical, mental, moral, habitual, and linguistic traits,[42] this notion became more specifically internal and narrow as scientists developed psychometric procedures in the mid-twentieth century. Few members of the public and few scientists noticed how success on intelligence tests required more than mental skill but rather also relied on attention, concentration, and comfort in formal testing settings within the presence of (white) authorities.[43] Lack of these habits in many blacks (as well as biased test construction, among other variables) may have caused significantly lower performance scores—a criterion used to distinguish racial groups and to attribute just rewards.

Two noteworthy figures worked simultaneously to counter fixed notions of race, particularly as they served to maintain racism and racial hierarchy. W. E. B. DuBois worked to overturn normative notions of biological race. He maintained the scientific talk of "blood" and "genius" but complicated race by describing deeper differences, including spiritual, social, and psychical differences between people.[44] In this way and others, DuBois fought against biological determinism—the inherent fixity that the intelligence testing movement upheld. Franz Boas, in a Deweyan spirit, also challenged racial categories by arguing that bodily habits are plastic and can change under environmental pressures. He guided anthropology away from studying fixed races toward studying cultures who share worldviews and temperament.[45]

With the discovery of the structure of DNA in 1953 and its subsequent mapping more recently, scientific understandings of race have changed dramatically. Despite a few exceptions,[46] most biologists and biological anthropologists agree that genetic analyses deny the existence of discrete racial categories. While certain geographic populations have been found to have some similar genetic proclivities, these populations do not break down along the lines most common people use to distinguish race in everyday parlance. Rather than members of each race sharing a unique genetic code, geneticists have actually shown that there is more genetic variation within culturally defined racial groups than between them.[47] These microanalyses have led most biologists to proclaim, as I stated at the outset of this chapter, that races do not exist. However, within the same time frame, many social and a small number of biological scientists have continued to investigate human differences in intelligence (namely, IQ), athletic ability, economic success, susceptibility to disease, and educational achievement within the context of distinct racial groups.

HABITS AND THE REALITY OF RACE TODAY

Despite proclamations of the "no-races" view by biologists, the general public continues to believe in the reality of race and to distinguish races at multiple levels: from formal job application check boxes to assessing strangers in a passing glance on the street. Pragmatist philosopher David McClean rightly notes, "Anything that tends to govern behavior—class, professional categories, etc.—and that may serve as an organizing or a unifying principle *is* real."[48] Most notably for my purposes here, such distinctions are often based on bodily habit. While the quickest glances of even children at an early age detect race from certain physical features, including skin color and facial features, far more nuanced understandings of the engaged body are often used to determine race. These habits and the meaning that are assigned to them guide behavior and organization, effectively making race real. John Warren explains, "If we look at race as a stylized repetition of acts, in which the gestures, movements, and other kinds of communication constitute meaning, then race as an identifier of difference is not *in* the body but rather made *through* bodily acts. This is to say, the repeated performance of race creates an illusion of substance that appears bodily."[49]

Stereotypes that are generally held of races within schools also display sensitivity to bodily action and to Deweyan habit insofar as they emphasize the predispositions of children to act in certain ways. One educational researcher notes the interpretation of native Hawaiian students in terms of corporeal activity—the way their bodies enact wildness, erratic behavior, and disrespect. Here, as was often the case in the scientific treatises I uncovered, the racial traits of the body are described in terms of lack, where a white standard operates without mention:

> The body of the average Hawaiian kid in school today—a student who is also likely to be from a poor or working class family—is read as inconsistent with the demands of the mind. That child . . . is likely to be described as "lack"—lack of discipline, a lack of respect for the things that really matter, lack of intellect, rationality, and initiative. His/her behavior is read ominously, as indicating a "wildness" that is threatening to the authority of school and to her/his own future well being as a "productive" member of society.[50]

Similarly, a white teacher notes the physical and behavioral proclivities of his Samoan students: "'Samoan students—' he shakes his head, smiling. . . . 'They are *wild*! Running around the halls. They seem to be good-hearted folk, but . . .'"[51]

Stereotypical images (including both bodily activity and other traits) of children of many different types of backgrounds, including races and nations, are well-known among teachers. Alan Peshkin notes of the high school he observed,

> Here is the picture teachers presented about their students. Asians, which include students from South and Southeast Asian nations, are polite, respectful,

formal, and obedient. They received uniformly high praise for their academic performance; though quiet in discussion, they always do their homework, work hard, want to succeed, and are attentive and persistent. White students seem to defy generalization. Filipino students were closer to other Asians than to non-Asians; yet, being more Americanized, they were less docile, formal, and obedient. While participating more in discussion and being active in asking questions, they did not exhibit the same intensity for academic success as Southeast Asians. They stood with the other Asians, however, in having high academic aspirations. Mexican students, generally formal, polite, and well-behaved, had relatively low academic motivation and high drop-out rates.[52]

He adds, "Teachers who felt they could generalize, most readily described black students. They were 'laid-back,' kidded more, liked physical contact, took criticism poorly, sought attention, and were rebellious and bold. Black girls were singled out as loud and aggressive, with a chip on their shoulders. Academically, black students had the desire but lacked foundations for learning, needed extra help, had short attention spans, and were hampered by speaking in black dialect. This picture does not apply to the small group of college-prep students."[53]

Contemporary American culture has named many race related habits in the context of black/white distinction: patterns of speech (Ebonics), movement (swaggers, jive, or dip), and performance (whiggers), to name only a few. People turn to these habitual markers to determine race, especially when confounded by lack of definitive surface-level physical features. Popular culture plays off them, with movies such as *Malibu's Most Wanted*, *Napoleon Dynamite*, and *White Chicks* depicting individuals of seemingly one surface-level race being perceived as another by virtue of comportment, ways of speaking, gestures, and the like. Moreover, the movie characters exaggerate certain activities, thereby highlighting the pertinence of their more subtle forms to interpreting and experiencing race. Formal institutions in the United States confront these racial habits by implementing educational policy regarding, for example, the acceptance and prohibition of Ebonics in classroom assignments and discussions.

Many students proclaim that others "act white" or "act black" and quickly explain that the person in question talks a certain way, is predisposed to certain activities, or relates to others in a particular style. One high school student, the president of the school's Samoan Club, expressed her struggles with these assessments from other students in a moving speech:

Tuli said she had to make an announcement, and if the bell rang, she didn't want anyone to leave. After a long pause and looking up at the ceiling, she said that she was resigning as president. "I will no longer be a part of the organization," she said. "I will be Tuli Jenkins, going to class, and getting an education. I'm tired of people saying 'you're acting too white,' 'you're acting too black,' 'you're not being the president.' Well, I'm not going to be a doormat. I can't do it no more. Nobody comes up to my face—I just hear Tuli this, Tuli that. All this talkin' shit—I can't take it. I just want to try to be a Samoan person—not too white, not too black," she said. She was still looking up at the ceiling, her eyes tearing, speaking in alternately measured and rushed speeds, shaking her head side to side. As others spoke in support of her, she moved to stand over by the corner. The last thing I remember her saying was: "People say 'you talk like your white, you got a black last name.' I can't take it any more." She finally did walk out.[54]

Students in this case and in many others note their skills at determining race according to how one acts. One high school student proudly reports the ability to decipher any other student's race on the basis of the way one talks, walks, or appears.[55] These assessments of race bear significant reality for students, including the very real possibility of being harmed given which race their bodily activities are perceived to display. Michael, a California high school student, told his teacher of a friend who was beat up on the bus because the other riders said he was acting white.[56] The racialized perception of his habits, then, had real consequences—consequences that might effectively reify the race itself. Punishments and threats for failing to be or act in line with the image of one's appropriate race reinforce that race as a real, natural entity. The experiences of this boy and of the distraught Samoan girl are certainly not uncommon throughout the United States and probably elsewhere.

When surveying another person, one does not say, "He appears white"; one says, "He *is* white." One's proclamations account for all the aspects of his being white[57] rather than simply his body, which is marked as white on the surface. It is interesting to note how these claims differ from the previous statement that "Michael acts white." "He is white" is used as though it mapped to some objective fact of reality that is true regardless of his activities. In fact, we have seen here that it is habitual activities that have come to define race in the first place. In contrast, to say that "he acts white" identifies an imposter, one who achieves (or fails at) a racial classification different from his "true" race by virtue of enacting whiteness.

The public maintains many of the ways in which science classified racial groups for centuries via habitual description and organization. Adopting the current "no-races" view is not enticing for many because it does not aid one in navigating a world where race continues to operate in everyday life. This view is not reconcilable with their experience of the world as organized by and sensitive to the habits of race. Letting go of a category that still has significant effects in the world is hardly persuasive to many people.

Many students struggle because they experience race as real, yet they hear slogans in school that deny race by touting the essential sameness of all people. Pollock, a high school teacher and educational researcher, recounts two events displaying such confliction:

> When a girl rose angrily out of the stands during a spirit rally in September 1996 and headed toward a player on the girls' soccer team roaring "I'm gonna kick your butt!," for example, Beaux, a black student who was sitting next to me and watching the interaction, yelled down an overtly racialized warning to the soccer player: "The Samoans are gonna get you!" "No," he added, smiling down at his feet, "we're all the same though." Students regularly parroted such popular clichés about how race should not matter ("can't we all get along?" was a prime example) at the same time that they were suggesting more explicitly that race *did* matter. Through such paradoxical citations, they similarly complicated popular arguments for the relevance of race. In October 1995, for example, I noticed several black students citing the overtly racialized statements of Louis Farrakhan's upcoming "Million Man March" in neatly double-edged tones: As people were sitting down during passing time between classes, an African-American boy came in and raised his fist, said "black power!," laughed, and walked out. Often laughing even as they publicly presented solemn gestures of racialized solidarity, students somehow managed to mock and broadcast race's importance simultaneously.[58]

While slogans of sameness may apply to some situations or to certain goals students or schools may hold, they often conflict with the everyday experience of racial difference, separation, and tension.

Smedley, a respected social constructionist, worries that the general public fails to distinguish acquired cultural behavior and physical features.[59] Certainly, as evidenced earlier in this chapter, scientists throughout the past few centuries have also had difficulty doing so. But perhaps the physical and the cultural are not so easily distinguishable. This would partly explain why the corporeal experience of felt race lingers within people and is read on their bodies. Many people proudly proclaim their racial identification. Such proclamations reflect a complex account of the way one feels comfortable in the world, the way one speaks or moves, the way one interprets the image in the mirror, and the way one chooses to interact with others they perceive as similar and different to themselves.[60] When habits of race are understood in a Deweyan sense, as constituting in large part the very beings that we are, it is evident that this ease of self-identification exhibits a compilation of inhabiting race—of living *in* one's habits.

Even while race may be socially constructed, such habit-based identifications can have real, positive effects. Racial identification can provide one a sense of self or be useful as a rallying cry or basis for requesting recognition from other groups. They can help us make sense of our experiences in the world and provide us with an effective filter for interpreting them. Additionally, strong and admirable traditions of racial identity have emerged from sharing a sense of self with others or from having experienced similar conditions (including oppression) in life. On the other hand, habits of race can come to be inhabited in stagnant ways that block people off from people of other racial groups or can construct a narrow understanding of "what counts" as the race they claim to be. A seeming reality of racial discreteness and related criteria for assessing this divisive system result. Struggles with the ease of inhabiting race, the reality of race, and maintaining racial boundaries appear in the case of the Samoan club president I described earlier. In that instance, Tuli is forced to reconcile her activities that appear non-Samoan to others and her own definition and felt experience of being Samoan.

PERCEIVING RACE IN SCHOOLS

Social constructionists need to address the ways in which racialized social labels, meaning, and corresponding normative value are constructed. As Bernard Boxill notes, social constructions can be intentional or unintentional.[61] Historically explaining the degree of intention guiding the social construction of race in science can illuminate the link between the concept of race and the normative hierarchy of racism that has come to accompany it. Put differently,

> The recognition of race as non-natural is presumed to be liberatory. . . . But it is seeming to me that race (together with racism and race privilege) is apparently *constructed as* something inescapable. And it makes sense that it would be, since such a construction would best serve those served by race and racism.[62]

Social constructionists need (as a few have) to move beyond the claim that race is a social construction to understanding the historical intention or use of the construct and its link to racism. Histories, like the one I have laid out here, help us understand not only *that* race is a social construction but also *how* and *why* it is.

The *how* aspect is, in part, evident in the way that scientists and everyday people have studied and demarcated races. Not only is the living of one's life as raced an activity of habit, but habits filter and organize our perceptions of race as well. In the history given previously, scientists are shown to be drawn to certain features of humans; they are sensitive to specific aspects of bodily activity or human variation and not others. These proclivities begin with early educational training in classification. This can occur as simply as through an exercise like the following recorded in one early elementary classroom:

> The teacher spread the photos out on the table and announced "OK, can you discover which of all these different people in these pictures most looks like you?" The children smile and reach for the photos, picking them up and showing them to each other. One boy, Joey (3, Asian), selects a photo of a dark-skinned girl wearing a red robe and announces, "Here's me!" at the top of his lungs. The teacher looks over to him and smiles, remarking, "No, honey, that's a little Black girl. Which people look like you?" Joey stares at her for a moment or two, then returns to his perusal of the photos. He offers no challenge to the teacher's decision, nor does he provide an explanation of his choice. . . . Trevor (3, white) finds a photo of a smiling man in ethnic German garb and proclaims, "I got me." The teacher verifies that his choice is "correct," then beams at him and says, "Good going, Trevor!" He grins back at her and leaps from the table. Joey continues his search, while Rita (3, white/Latina) sorts through the pictures with him. Sarah (4, white) remains sitting quietly, swinging her legs under the table and looking bored. She makes no effort to look at the photos. Joey finds a photo of a group of smiling white women and silently offers it to Sarah. She studies it for a moment, then sighs and hands it to the teacher expectantly. "Good job, Sarah," the teacher congratulates her, not noticing that Joey produced this racial identification for Sarah. Sarah finally smiles and leaves the table. The entire exercise seems, to her, to be more an annoyance than a fun activity. Joey finds yet another photo, this time of a Native American man. He hands it to the teacher, smiling and announcing, "Finally. That looks like me." The teacher accepts this one and tells Joey that he made "a good match." He lets out his breath in a big puff and erupts from his chair. The teacher is left with Rita, who sits helplessly looking at the spread-out collection of photos. "Here's one," the teacher remarks, offering a photo of a woman in traditional Mexican garb to Rita. The little girl looks at it for a moment, smiles, and says sweetly, "Oh, such a pretty dress. Yes, that's me." The teacher beams at her, and the child asks, "Can I go now?"[63]

Here, children learn how to identify and categorize themselves and other children by drawing parallels between specific aspects of pictured people and themselves. Exercises as simple as this develop into learning how to construct complex schemata like Blumenbach's taxonomy. The training of a habit-based lens for perceiving race is affected by social standards regarding which types of groupings are significant or necessary. In both scientific and general settings, they learn that sorting and intricate analysis of variation can be academically and culturally worthwhile. Scientists develop habits that lead them to carry out certain sorting activities and to share their findings with others.

The habitual ways in which one perceives others who are different from oneself may be problematic. Habits may be narrow or limited, as is the case of white children who are unable to see the complexity and variation of color in skin and palms of their black peers[64] or the white boys in the British school mentioned earlier who do not see the athletic proficiencies of their South Asian peers whom they only see as slow and weak. In these cases, the white children's habits of perception show a tendency to homogenize others and to overlook differences within those groups as well as contradictions between their observations of a group and the beliefs they already hold about that group.

Habits may display an aversion to the new and different, thereby distorting perception or tainting it toward certain ends. In a Deweyan sense of habits as working capacities that give rise to desires, they may work hand in hand with a desire to establish and maintain one's own perceived superiority over the new person encountered. They may entail tendencies toward dominance, as evidenced in one school by a white girl, April, who grabs and screams at black students.[65] Habits of aversion often carry with them a history of previous exchanges with others of difference that the subject has experienced firsthand or has learned from others.

These habits lead one to act in certain ways, including, all too often in the case of racial difference, acting with hostility, fear, or aggression. Many theorists have described racism in terms of the beliefs of individuals or groups and the effects of systems of oppression. Few have considered how racism grows out of habits affecting race perception that have been honed over time, including some that have been born or shaped in schools. These habits influence how we think about other people and how we devise and use racial concepts to describe them. As habitual in the Deweyan sense, these ways of processing and interacting with the world are often automatic, occurring without thought or conscious intention. Unlike theorists who see racism as a belief or viewpoint wielded as a judgment carried out on or against others, Dewey rightly contends that, in most cases, "prejudice is not a judgment at all."[66] Or, as Linda Martín Alcoff says of racial perception, "our experience of habitual perceptions is so attenuated as to skip the stage of conscious interpretation and intent. Indeed, interpretation is the wrong word here: we are simply perceiving."[67] Hence, the very person who employs and is composed of these "racist" habits may herself deny or fail to see that she is racist. Racism is composed of bad habits insofar as they are often not conscious, have a hold over us, or, in many cases, lead us to do things for which we would otherwise be ashamed. These bad habits prevent ethical and fruitful interaction with others. The most outspoken racists—white supremacists and others like them—are a notable exception. In their case, they often are conscious of their racist habits. Even though conscious, however, they are still bad habits because they rigidly prevent one from keeping up with the multicultural world and from interacting with others in ethical or mutually beneficial ways.

Even in the absence of institutional or attitudinal racism, faulty habits of racial perception may linger. This suggests that racial tension will remain as long as problematic habits of perceiving others, such as those just described, are left intact. A closer analysis of these proclivities, guided by a Deweyan account of transaction, might aid us in revealing the environmental (including political, historical, normative, and economical) conditions that support and perpetuate race insofar as they impact our habits related to perception. Hence, they might begin to fill in the *why* aspect of race's social construction.

DETERMINING RACE IN THE FUTURE

Popular and scientific discourses of race, categories of difference, and criteria of hierarchy have impacted one another in intriguing ways throughout the history of modern Western science. Notably, bodily habits, rather than mere physical attributes, have served as major markers of racial difference and identity. These habits remain active within the general population even though scientists have proclaimed the unreality of race. Rather than continuing to simply push a "no-races" message, scientists, social constructionists, and teachers might more productively explore how habits continue to define and perpetuate race. Moreover, an investigation of habit may provide a better understanding of how races materialize and appear as though real on the flesh and within one's actions. This historical analysis depicts the staying power of race and, unlike the views of Naomi Zack, Kwame Appiah, Noel Ignatiev, and others who have rushed to call for the elimination of race, that race will linger.

Reworking popular understandings of racial habits in ways that reveal their transactive relationship with the environment might well incorporate and reflect recent advances in biological and genetic science. The contingency of one's habits—their dependence on environment and social group— echoes contemporary scientific claims about human variation statistically occurring across geographical populations based on chance mutations that have affected genetic structures within those groups rather than difference being based in innate races. The study of habits, as uniquely coconstituted by biological material and environmental transaction, may also offer insight into understanding how genetic codes are activated by environmental influences. Similarly, the study of habits, as inseparably biological and environmental, may confound genetic determinism, thereby troubling both legitimate genetic predictions and faulty determinist arguments of eugenicists.[68] Finally, in terms of biological and popular classification, renowned scientist Joseph Graves rightly claims that "the criteria upon which a classification scheme is based will necessarily affect the structure of that scheme."[69] When the criteria of classification are transactive racial habits that can be educationally cultivated and changed, the structure of the classificatory scheme will necessarily become more flexible and less rigid.

NOTES

1. Debra Van Ausdale and Joe R. Feagin, *The First R: How Children Learn Race and Racism* (Lanham, Md.: Rowman & Littlefield, 2001), 60–65.

2. By focusing on habit as a marker of race, I do not want to suggest that race is perceived only at the level of habit. I acknowledge that bodily surfaces (including colors, shapes, and textures) as well as economics, religious views, and other factors affect the categorization of race.

3. Judith Butler drawing on Foucault in *Gender Trouble: Tenth Anniversary Edition* (New York: Routledge, 1999), xxix.

4. Paul Connolly, *Racism, Gender Identities, and Young Children* (London: Routledge, 1998), 119.

5. Connolly, *Racism, Gender Identities, and Young Children*, 119–34.

6. Egyptian hieroglyph "The Great Hymn to Atem," quoted in Vincent Sarich and Frank Miele, *Race: The Reality of Human Differences* (Boulder, Colo.: Westview Press, 2004), 35.

7. Robert E. Kuttner, ed., *Race and Modern Science* (New York: Social Science Press, 1967), xv.

8. Audrey Smedley, *Race in North America: Origin and Evolution of a Worldview* (Boulder, Colo.: Westview Press, 1993), 52–61.

9. Smedley, *Race in North America*, 107.

10. Cornel West, *Keeping Faith: Philosophy and Race in America* (New York: Routledge, 1993).

11. Ira Berlin, "Time, Space, and the Evolution of Afro-American Society on British Mainland North America," *American Historical Review* 85, no. 1 (1980): 72.

12. Cornel West, *Keeping Faith: Philosophy and Race in America* (New York: Routledge, 1993).

13. Thomas F. Gossett, *Race: The History of an Idea in America* (Dallas: Southern Methodist University Press, 1963), 39; Londa Schiebinger, "The Anatomy of Difference: Race and Sex in Eighteenth Century Science," *Eighteenth Century Studies* 23, no. 4 (1990): 390.

14. Schiebinger, "The Anatomy of Difference," 393–94; Georges-Louis Leclerc de Buffon, "Histoire Naturelle," in *Oeuvres Completes de Buffon*, ed. Comte de Lacepède (Paris, 1818), 5 and 520; Johann Blumenbach, *On the Natural Varieties of Mankind*, trans. Thomas Bendyshe (1775; reprint, New York: Bergman Publishers, 1969), 116 and 240.

15. Gossett, *Race*, 40.

16. Joseph L. Graves, *The Emperor's New Clothes: Biological Theories of Race at the Millennium* (New Brunswick, N.J.: Rutgers University Press, 2001), 39.

17. Stuart Gilman, "Degeneracy and Race in the Nineteenth Century: The Impact of Clinical Medicine," *Journal of Ethnic Studies* 10, no. 4 (1983): 30.

18. Graves, *The Emperor's New Clothes*, 40.

19. Gossett, *Race*, 40.

20. Gossett, *Race*, 46.

21. Robert E. Bieder describes the intentions of white leaders in "Scientific Attitudes toward Indian Mixed-Bloods in Early Nineteenth Century America," *Journal of Ethnic Studies* 8, no. 2 (1980): 19.

22. Van Ausdale and Feagin, *The First R*, 142.

23. R. C. Lewontin, Steven Rose, and Leon J. Kamin, "IQ: The Rank Ordering of the World," in *The "Racial" Economy of Science: Toward a Democratic Future*, ed. Sandra Harding (Bloomington: Indiana University Press, 1993), 147.

24. Lewontin et al., "IQ," 148.

25. Sarich and Miele, *Race*, 71.

26. Nancy Stepan, *The Idea of Race in Science* (Hamden, Conn.: Archon Books, 1982), 25.

27. Francis Galton, *Hereditary Genius: An Inquiry into Its Laws and Consequences* (1869; reprint, New York: Horizon Press, 1952), 336.

28. Frederick L. Hoffman, *Race Traits and Tendencies of the American Negro* (New York: Macmillan, 1896).

29. Anne Fausto-Sterling describes these measurements in, "Gender, Race, and Nation: The Comparative Anatomy of 'Hottentot' Women in Europe, 1815–1817," in *Deviant Bodies*, ed. Jennifer Terry and Jacqueline Urla (Bloomington: Indiana University Press, 1995), 31.

30. David R. Roediger, *Wages of Whiteness: Race and the Making of the American Working Class* (London: Verso, 1991), 97 and 105.

31. Gossett, *Race*, 155.

32. Sarich and Miele, *Race*, 80.

33. Smedley, *Race in North America*, 265.

34. Stephen Jay Gould, *The Mismeasure of Man* (New York: Norton, 1981), 77.

35. Smedley, *Race in North America*, 264.

36. Charles Darwin, *The Origin of Species by Means of Natural Selection; Or, the Preservation of Favoured Races in the Struggle for Life* (1859; reprint, London: Penguin, 1968), 239.

37. Charles Darwin, *The Origin of Species by Means of Natural Selection* (1859; reprint, New York: Modern Library, 1936), 547. Note that here I am using the labels of superiority and inferiority, which Darwin himself uses.

38. Charles Darwin, *The Descent of Man and Selection in Relation to Sex* (1871; reprint, New York: D. Appleton and Company, 1896), 68.

39. Charles Darwin, *The Descent of Man and Selection in Relation to Sex* (1871; reprint, New York: Modern Library, 1936), 536.

40. In *The Origin of Species*, Darwin describes his early encounters with enslaved Africans and is deeply troubled by the way they keep their eyes to the ground and shield themselves from seemingly deserved blows from their masters—as though their bodies reveal their inferiority and submissiveness in every regard.

41. Stanley Fish, "Reverse Racism, or How the Pot Got to Call the Kettle Black," in *Affirmative Action: Social Justice or Race Discrimination*, ed. F. Beckwith and T. Jones (Amherst, N.Y.: Prometheus, 1997).

42. Public Broadcasting System, http://www.pbs.org/race/ 000_About/002_04-back ground-01.htm (accessed April 2, 2004).

43. Lewontin et al., "IQ," 147.

44. Julia E. Liss, "Diasporic Identities: The Science and Politics of Race in the Work of Franz Boas and W. E. B. DuBois, 1894–1919," *Cultural Anthropology* 13, no. 2 (1998): 132.

45. Liss, "Diasporic Identities," 139; Sarich and Miele, *Race*, 87.

46. Sarich and Miele, to name just two, in *Race*.

47. This means that if a group of "white"-appearing people were compared to a group of "Asian"-appearing people, there is likely to be greater genetic variation among the members of each of these two groups as there would be if the groups were compared to each other in their entirety.

48. David E. McClean, "Should We Conserve the Notion of Race?," in *Pragmatism and the Problem of Race*, ed. Bill E. Lawson and Donald F. Koch (Bloomington: Indiana University Press, 2004), 147.

49. John T. Warren, *Performing Purity: Whiteness, Pedagogy, and the Reconstruction of Power* (New York: Peter Lang, 2003), 29.

50. Gail Masuchika Boldt, "Failing Bodies: Discipline and Power in Elementary Classrooms," *Journal of Curriculum Theorizing* 17, no. 4 (2001): 100.

51. Mica Pollock, *Colormute: Race Talk Dilemmas in an American School* (Princeton, N.J.: Princeton University Press, 2004), 155.

52. Alan Peshkin, *Color of Strangers, the Color of Friends* (Chicago: University of Chicago Press, 1991), 148.

53. Peshkin, *Color of Strangers, the Color of Friends*, 149.

54. Pollock, *Colormute*, 30.

55. Pollock, *Colormute*, 24–25.

56. Pollock, *Colormute*, 52.

57. Often people will conveniently overlook aspects of the person being examined that appear out of sync with their initial perception of his or her race in order to categorize him or her neatly within a discrete group.

58. Pollock, *Colormute*, 48–49.

59. Smedley, *Race in North America*, 13.

60. Consider an example of self-identification of race that showed a certain sense of comfort in inhabiting and identifying one's race (especially relative to someone of a different race) at even a young age. "Del (4, Black) wrestles Travis (4, white) to the ground. Del is large for his age, closer to the size of a six-year-old. He sits on Travis's chest, loudly announcing, 'Stay down there, you. I'm Black; I'm powerful. I'm Black. I'm strong.' Travis's face screws up, ready to cry." Van Ausdale and Feagin, *The First R*, 114.

61. Bernard Boxill, ed., *Race and Racism* (New York: Oxford University Press, 2001), 30.

62. Marilyn Frye, "White Woman Feminist 1983–1992," in *Race and Racism*, ed. Bernard Boxill (New York: Oxford University Press, 2001), 86.

63. Van Ausdale and Feagin, *The First R*, 52–53.

64. Van Ausdale and Feagin, *The First R*, 61.

65. Van Ausdale and Feagin, *The First R*, 112.

66. John Dewey, "Racial Prejudice and Friction," in *The Middle Works of John Dewey*, vol. 13, ed. Jo Ann Boydston (1921; reprint, Carbondale: Southern Illinois University Press, 1988), 243.

67. Linda Martín Alcoff, "Habits of Hostility: On Seeing Race," *Philosophy Today*, 44 (suppl. 2000): 32.

68. Note Davenport's call for the future of eugenics in genetic determinism, a movement still supported under similar ideals today in some small circles: *"The great work of the future in eugenics is to determine as accurately as possible the law of heredity of each human trait."* Charles Davenport, "The Eugenics Programme and Progress in Its Achievement," in *Eugenics: Twelve University Lectures* (New York: Dodd, Mead, 1914), 7 (italics in original).

69. Graves, *The Emperor's New Clothes*, 37.

Chapter Four

Redoing Gender with Judith Butler

Michael, an early elementary student in Ohio, curiously admired a container of nail polish he and his classmates found among his teacher's belongings. Although the other children were girls, Michael decided that he, too, wanted to try painting his nails. He enjoyed seeing the bright red polish decorate his fingers. It was not until Michael returned to school the next day that the nail polish raised concern. Michael presented his teacher a note from his father, who angrily asked that Michael no longer be given nail polish. Michael, apparently echoing words he had heard from his father, exclaimed, "I'm a good boy!" and "boys don't wear nail polish." Even though the teacher agreed that boys do not *usually* wear nail polish, Michael persisted with his exclamations. Feeling as though he had not convinced his teacher, he pulled down his pants and shouted, "I am a boy!"[1]

Judith Butler's intriguing work over the past decade can help explain how children like Michael become gendered; how they use cues, like nail polish and penises, to demarcate gender; and how they experiment with performing gender differently. Many contemporary poststructural and feminist accounts of gender and identity display parallels to the interpretation of Dewey's work that I have offered in the previous two chapters. In this chapter, I spell out some of those similarities by focusing on Butler in particular. I highlight her work because she has painstakingly and provocatively detailed the process of gender materialization and its political ramifications in ways that both extend and complicate the Deweyan-inspired sense of racial identity I have illustrated up to this point. I describe her theory of gender identity, noting points of both similarity and difference to the Deweyan theory of habit that I used to depict racial formation and performance. I explain the possibility for political agency that arises from Butler's account of subjectivity and elucidate some of the political acts that can or should follow from this possibility. Adopting these political acts alongside a Deweyan account of habit begins to suggest directions for how problematic identities and moments of racial and gender conflict might be transformed. Throughout this discussion, I refer to actual classroom situations to depict gender formation, performance, and change from Butler's perspective.

BECOMING A SUBJECT, BECOMING GENDERED

In much the same way that Dewey's accounts of identity and agency begin with the transactive life of the organism, Butler's theories of gender and agency follow from her portrayal of the discursive process of becoming an embodied subject. In Butler's view, bodies are neither natural nor prelinguistic. They are not simply biological entities that exist regardless of their surroundings. Instead, bodies are linguistically constituted and socially constructed. It is our social and language systems that make a person real and significant. This means that "as a locus of cultural interpretations, the body is a material reality which has already been located and defined within a social context."[2] Bodies acquire meaning and significance via the language that labels them and affects their activities. Bodies do not exist as passively removed from the world around them; rather, meaning is inscribed on them, and they impart influence on their surroundings. The human body is a construction, but, responding to Foucault, Butler insists that the body is not simply a preexisting surface on which cultural meaning is inscribed from without.[3] While discourse may produce the illusion of a bound surface to be passively inscribed and read, the body is actually an active and whole being capable of performance and ritual.

The body comes into being through enacting recognizable human behavior, like being feminine or black. It becomes a subject when it is interpellated—when it is labeled and addressed by someone in a position of power—as a recognizable person of certain normalized identity traits. When a teacher exclaims to a new kindergartner who has just politely presented a gift, "My what a kind, sweet, little girl you are!," the child is (re)inducted into the linguistic world as a character displaying certain (in many cases socially desirable) female traits. Because the child has displayed admirable traits of femininity, she is interpellated as a girl, and her existence as female is confirmed. To become a subject of speech and a legitimate social actor, one must embody the social norms that govern speech and social participation, thereby making one intelligible. Or, in Butler's words, "to embody the norms that govern speakability in one's speech is to consummate one's status as a subject of speech."[4] Bodies and performativity have meaning as signs and signification that allow them to be culturally recognized. The body does not have materiality until it serves as a signifier, expressing recognizable traits. Learning and displaying social norms, an activity that children perform from birth and that is particularly emphasized in schools, is an embodied activity and the process of materialization.[5] We see Michael struggling through this process as he seeks legitimation for his masculine body from his teacher after invoking conflicting signs.

Drawing on Foucault's theory of power as productive, Butler describes a process of discursive construction, where the circulating power of cultural norms and practices brings the subject into being and produces the effect of a bounded, identity-marked, material body. Gender, race, and other embodied identity categories are the effects of activities and styles of being read on the body by others and performed by and internalized within oneself. For instance, American cultural (though typically unstated) mandates about the way a man greets another man style his bodily activity such that he is recognized as a man when he shakes another's right hand firmly. Because they are continually and repetitively reinstated, identity categories and traits appear stable and inherent, as though men are naturally forward and strong. Hence, gender is an effect rather than an internal essence.[6] Gender is also a norm that, while not completely reducible to its instantiations, is maintained by perpetual acts, like hand shaking, that continually define and idealize gender in daily life.

Through continual repetition of identity defining acts and being interpellated by others, a stable subject with an apparently coherent identity results. The subject is forced to continue the performance of such an identity in order to maintain its constitution as a viable being—to have a social position that is recognized and that affords the subject the ability to speak and be heard. For Butler, performativity is the repetition of cultural norms and codes, the activity of which styles and constitutes us because it has the ability to produce what it names. The traits and identities imparted are then sustained through bodily comportment and the continued force of cultural structures. Traits that appear natural or as essences, like gender, come from without with such force and constancy that they appear as though internally sprung, and their seeming naturalness goes largely unquestioned. Typically, we do not knowingly perform such reiterations but rather must do so in order to maintain our existence within their constraints. Over time, the resulting gender becomes sedimented—as though a natural, original, and immutable characteristic.

In the case of Michael and the nail polish, we see a young boy's efforts to make sense of his gender coherence. He struggles with the coherence of his gendered activities and the impact of these acts on his status as materially male and as a viable boy among his friends and family. His father has induced or bolstered the fear of jeopardizing his masculine status by engaging in activities that may lead to gender ambiguity and hence may teeter on linguistic unintelligibility. By failing to uphold the gendered norms of play and adornment, he risks losing the discursive support that sustains him as a viable male subject. Again and again, the student proclaims that "I am a boy" until his status is confirmed by the teachers. Still uncertain that his masculinity has been fully acknowledged, he resorts to the defining act of displaying his genitals, which he seems to envision as essentially and unequivocally masculine.[7]

BUTLER ON AGENCY

The subject is compelled to perform identity constraints and cite norms, and it is in this regard that Butler breaks from her humanist forerunners, including many pragmatists. Working against the notion of a prediscursive agent who *chooses* to do a deed, Butler shows that the subject *must* performatively repeat these norms in order to maintain its status as a recognizable human. The subject is intimately wrapped in power webs that constrain it and prevent a substantial sense of voluntary agency. Importantly, however, Butler adds that this nonhumanist subject is not entirely culturally determined and that, even though constructed, the very circulations of power that constitute the subject render it capable of agency.[8] Butler, here, is also responding to her structuralist counterparts who also describe subject construction but who, because they posit that it is an event that happens once and for all, deny the possibility of agency and radical change of cultural structures.

Working within the discursive constraints that constitute us, Butler locates the body as a source of initiative and change. While the body is never entirely within one's grasp, the embodied subject has the capacity for agency. Counterintuitively, Butler asks, "What possibilities exist *by virtue of* the constructed character of sex and gender?"[9] Butler responds that we do not lose agency by virtue of being constructed; rather, she claims that the process of construction confers the ability to will and produce effects in the world because it renders us intelligible and linguistically viable.[10]

Within linguistic confines, "the question of *agency* is reformulated as a question of how signification and resignification work."[11] When identity is understood as the signification of political signs, agency becomes resignification and variation of necessary repetition and is capable of revealing signification as never fully fixed or determined. People have the ability to change how they are constituted and the social forces that influence their constitution by varying repetition via embodied response to interpellation. Responding in unpredictable ways, or misappropriating the label placed on oneself, calls into question the meaning and applicability of that label—tossing it into the limelight as unnatural or problematic, if only for a moment. For instance, in one high school, a Filipino-appearing student misappropriates the term used to label him and deploys it in unusual ways. The boy is speaking to two black guys when he notes, "I know who's a niggapino—my auntie. And that one guy, he's a niggapino; my cousin's a pino; she's [points across room] a japapino."[12] His play on the "pinos" term suggests that the term lacks nuance or accuracy for describing complex identities. This sense of agency is not self-determination—as though the boy could suddenly determine what term others should use to label him—but the ability to challenge the social customs in which one is necessarily situated. It is, for this student, the ability to trouble the terms of identity by which he must be described in order to receive recognition. Through subverting cultural law, "the culturally constructed body will then be liberated, neither to its 'natural' past, nor to its original pleasures, but to an open future of cultural possibilities."[13] For the boy who plays with the term "pinos," this is a future where racial identities have a wider variety of possible meanings and suitable antecedents. Given the construction of identity, then, agency is the ability to construct differently.

The subject's exploitation of the unstable language that constitutes him or her is often spontaneous and unpredictable. Because linguistic subjects are necessarily constrained within cultural norms and practices, Butler believes that the subject cannot achieve the critically reflective distance necessary for analyzing and intentionally changing one's identity performances. Acts of subversion, then, are generally not carried out by one who reflects on them and then consciously chooses to act but, rather, occur by virtue of a subject's being located in a certain web of power, at a certain moment, and by behaving in ways that cannot be fully predetermined. Linguistic and political insurrection is spawned in minute instances of power redeployment rather than transcendence. Such insurrection is capable of producing significant effects over time insofar as it reveals the problematically constructed nature of identity-defined life and difficulties with the social institutions that support it. Performatives are provisionally successful not because they emit from a subject's intention but because they bear a history of authority through their citations of established practices.[14] Butler's agent, then, wields neither sovereign power nor intention. Agency is an effect and redeployment of power rather than a property of a person.

AGENCY AND POLITICAL INSURRECTION

Given Butler's account of the process of becoming an agent, certain exercises of agency as political protest and change follow. While keeping in mind that the success of political insurrection is always provisional according to Butler,[15] subject construction and its inherent acts of violence and exclusion call for insurrection. Most proponents of identity politics or multicultural education would also be troubled by these violent and exclusionary acts. They typically respond by championing minority rights and by demanding just recognition of minority races and genders. Butler and most of her poststructuralist colleagues, however, call for political action that fights against violence and exclusion by ultimately rejecting all identity categories. Even while she grants that identity categories can be used strategically in some contexts, her overarching goal is for gender (and all other hierarchical identity categories) to be "overthrown, eliminated, or rendered fatally ambiguous."[16]

Exposing the Failures of a Cohesive Identity

When subjects are interpellated and forced to repeat cultural constraints or are ushered into the distinct identity groups, they continually define and reinforce a boundary of which types of life and living are acceptable and which are not. Identity categories, then, are not merely harmless descriptions of bodily appearance or even activity. Rather, they are normative insofar as they entail standards of exclusion and inclusion. In this way, hierarchies of identity and living and, moreover for Butler, alterity are established. While unspoken and largely unimaginable, a realm of exclusion is constructed and maintained as that opposed to which identity-based living is defined. Those who do not fulfill cultural standards or who fail to uphold viable interpellations are relegated to this realm of exclusion and are often retained there through violent acts.[17] They are silenced, and alternative ways of living and being are foreclosed.

Although we can never achieve total inclusivity of what counts as human (because categories always have boundaries), we can work toward producing resignifications that reveal exclusions and draw in those previously excluded. Butler urges us to work toward connections and against exclusions. Democracy and associated ways of living become more radically inclusive for Butler when terms of exclusion (like "queer") are affirmed by discursive outliers, enabling them to return to the realm of discussion.

Additionally, agency can expose the failures of cultural norms to achieve their goals, including the normative aim of cohesive, unified identity. While other theorists, including many multicultural educators, seek to determine or celebrate the most essential and permanent aspects of a person that determine his or her identity, Butler inquires into the problematically constraining features of such activities by asking,

> To what extent do *regulatory practices* of gender formation and division constitute identity, the internal coherence of the subject, indeed, the self-identical status of the person? To what extent is "identity" a normative ideal rather than a descriptive feature of experience? And how do the regulatory practices that govern gender also govern culturally intelligible notions of identity?[18]

Indeed, when discussing gender with her class one day, Gail Masuchika Boldt, a teacher and educational researcher, noted that her students easily and in agreement provided a list of appropriate gender traits that comprised a coherent gender ideal. Boldt remarks,

> My students are not wholly describing any of themselves individually; rather, they are describing an *"idealized gender identity."* For my students, the expectation exists that there is something real that it means to be a boy and something that it means to be a girl.[19]

Often these idealized gender identities are shored up through educational materials, like stories and mathematical word problems, that confirm them. In other cases they are reinforced by the continuous divisive practices of teachers who address their students as "boys and girls" and who separate them into gendered lines, physical education groups, or study buddies. More than simple description of gendered people, these idealized identities become perpetual practices of regulation. They shape people into certain normative notions of gender and provide them a coherent sense of gendered self that often omits the inconsistent ways one fails to always uphold a gender ideal.

Striving for identity coherence requires that one continually distinguish oneself from the abject who has been excluded from one's identity category, thereby causing distance and differentiation rather than connection between people. This differentiating activity occurs daily at individual and institutional levels in one setting that Butler largely overlooks: schools. There, many children learn the practice of exclusion through learning how to categorize themselves and others. This is most obvious in the example I recounted earlier where young children must locate photos of people with distinctly typed race, ethnicity, and gender who resemble themselves. As this activity plays out, we see some children assisting their peers by identifying the "correct" choice for others, thereby learning to distinguish not only themselves but children of other races and genders as well. One biracial white/Latina girl struggles with this activity until she is finally ushered into a Mexican identification by her teacher. Even in the moment of acceptance, the girl interestingly identified with the beauty of the pictured woman's dress rather than her racial or ethnic appearance, thereby preventing the differentiation and perhaps derogatory interpellation of the teacher from fully taking hold.

Van Ausdale and Feagin also relay one of many other pertinent examples. They describe an afternoon recess event. Renee (white) pulls Lingmai (Asian) and Jocelyn (white) in a wagon:

> Eventually, Renee drops the handle, and Lingmai jumps from the wagon and picks up the handle. As Lingmai begins to pull, Renee admonishes her, "No, No. You can't pull this wagon. Only white Americans can pull this wagon."[20]

Here Renee, in order to maintain her sense of white Americans as physically strong and leaders, must once again position Lingmai outside this coherent ring of traits. Rather than simply an act based on racist beliefs of Asian inferiority, this event is part of a normative process of identity construction and maintenance carried out performatively. This prevents the girls from achieving fully interactive and equal play. Some educators would mistakenly propose an antibias curriculum aimed at sensitizing these girls to their supposed racially biased beliefs. While potentially bringing about some benefits, success of this curriculum is likely to be quite limited. Other educators might promote inclusiveness by instituting a "you can't say 'you can't play'" type of rule, which is also likely to have limited success.[21] The problem might more appropriately be assuaged, however, if these girls learned about the exclusionary practices of identity and how they mold one's body, desires, and interactions as well as how to exploit them. Teachers should help these children see how the discursive formation of their identities could be improved by no longer disavowing difference in the Butlerian sense but rather through coordinated transaction across difference, as I further explain in chapter 6.

Drawing on Slavoj Zizek and Jacques Lacan, Butler argues that identity categories never achieve their intended unity. Rather, a space of indeterminacy is left open where subjects may ponder or display the ways in which they do not fit under certain identity labels. Symbolic law and norms may be called into question by failing to perform as a uniform subject or by revealing how the law has created more than it intended.[22] The subject-agent may also call to attention the acts of differentiation that continually distinguish identity groups. Lingmai, then, might have displayed white American traits by aggressively assuming wagon pulling duty as rightfully her own or may have pointed out that the implications regarding her in Renee's claim not only were inaccurate but also made the game unfair by unequally distinguishing the girls.

Competing Identity Categories

Some people never achieve intelligibility because they do not fit into coherent norms of gender, race, or other forms of identity that define or confer recognition.[23] These are people who perhaps display ambiguous racial or gender characteristics or do not behave consistently in ways that are identifiable with distinct identity categories. Butler provides the example of David/Brenda, who was born with XY chromosomes but given surgery and raised as female. Her body and her activities are often gender ambiguous, and she is both ignored and attacked by her school peers in different settings.[24] Her classmates are unable to make sense of her gender or form language to convey it. They result to violently excluding her from masculinity and threatening her life if she fails to comply to the norms of femininity, like sitting to urinate in the school bathroom.

While largely invisible to most people and unable to achieve viability in the world, these unintelligible outliers, like David/Brenda, are the required foils that put common and normative identities in relief. While these positions are problematic because they are denied a space for efficacy in the world and the protection of identity-based rights, Butler suggests that inhabiting them is not necessarily a bad thing when the norms defining intelligibility are unjust or harmful. Those outside the realm of intelligibility are able to reflect on these norms and recognize their injurious capacities.[25] This slight advantage does not, however, warrant the continued violent exclusion of those outliers. Increasing the possibilities for acceptable gender is a necessity of social and linguistic justice in Butler's view because those who are currently excluded need those possibilities to be recognized in order to achieve life and viability, including, for David/Brenda, the ability to participate fully as him-/herself in school without the threat of annihilation.[26] While this is in part a process of forming new genders, it is largely the inclusion of those already existing variations, like David/Brenda's. Butler presents this challenge to those agents already working on the boundaries of intelligibility, exposing their permeability and their faulty attempts at maintaining normative coherence.

One way of working against exclusion and coherence is to corrupt identity categories or render them ambiguous. They should not, however, be prematurely denied or erased because they are necessary for cultural existence and the signification of certain states of living (such as "woman" as subordination or a list of sexual attributes). At present, these categories are still necessary for helping us make sense of the world or for seeking group rights. Butler's sense of agency appreciates the democratic political potential of these categories as open and contested and encourages subjects to invoke the categories, especially as terms of affiliation for political action, while simultaneously critiquing them. Rallying cries like "Black Power!" that Pollock witnesses in her classroom can positively unite students in solidarity or in efforts to secure equal rights, but such proclamations should be interrogated to see who does or does not count as black and the like. Indeed, her students set the stage for such interrogations when a Filipino boy, with playful mockery, holds out his fist and exclaims "Filipino!" shortly after a black student has raised her fist and powerfully asserted "I—am—Black!"[27] "The goal for Butler and other poststructuralists interested in intersections of identity and politics," as summed up by Robert Brookey and Diane Miller, "is not to describe who we 'really' are, because such a description would be impossible. Instead, they seek to identify the means through which we can best articulate our identities in order to achieve our political goals" and, ultimately, I would add, to reject all identity categories.[28]

Butler encourages the adoption of identity categories in new ways that change the traditional definitions. She aims for a "crossroads" connecting identity positions out of acknowledgment of their founding and continuous acts of exclusion. She envisions this space as one of connection and resignification of identity terms, where possibilities can be expanded without perpetuating differentiation and exclusion. Those working toward this crossroads can reveal the false uniformity attributed to individual identity categories like gender and race by showing how they are imbricated in one another rather than distinct.[29] Butler promotes the shifting of identity positions not because one comes to recognize how they are similarly constituted at the moment but because one acknowledges the acts of exclusion that have led to those identity categories and one, therefore, seeks connection across them. Schools could well be equipped to do this kind of tracing. History classes, for example, might show how Irish and blacks were similarly disavowed as savage in order to shore up the image of whiteness. The class may then serve as a space where children from each of these categories try out and rework those identity positions with this new knowledge.

Speaking in New Ways

Butler is particularly sensitive to the use of speech to define and differentiate identity categories. She urges justice-conscious people to speak in new ways and to resignify old terms. Current identity category names may be employed but should be used in ways that reveal and rework their exclusionary aims. Referring to a perlocutionary view of language, Butler identifies the gap between the utterance and its effects as a space for resignification. During that interval, words like "nigger" or "fag" that harmfully describe or label identity categories may take on new meanings, be taken up in new contexts, or be contested in ways that disjoin the word from its power to injure. Although the repetition of injurious speech inflicts continued trauma, the space between repetitions may vary the next utterance in slightly different ways, modes, or locations. Thereby, iterability partially breaks the force of the word from its historicity. While admitting that repetition may preserve as well as subvert past meanings, Butler locates the ability to contest injurious speech in these moments. Addressing harmful speech is best done through resignification rather than censorship. Indeed, she notes

> that such language carries trauma is not a reason to forbid its use. There is no purifying language of its traumatic residue, and no way to work through trauma except through the arduous effort it takes to direct the course of its repetition.[30]

Butler suggests that the link between word and wound may be broken or disrupted. Public misappropriation and recontextualization of words can trouble their meanings and their ability to produce certain effects. The dependency of damaging identity words on performance—relying on repetition and systems of oppression—can be revealed as a vulnerability when the repetition takes unexpected twists that diffuse its virility. Biased words can be reclaimed slowly over time by the groups they negatively portray or by others who contest them, as has happened with the word "queer."

In the following conversation, we see a powerful reworking of an identity category intended to harm. Educational researcher Paul Connolly (PC) recorded the following British classroom conversation between five- and six-year-olds Jordan (biracial, white/West Indian), who struggles to maintain his identity as black and of Jamaican descent among his peers, and Stephen (biracial, Pakistani/black?):

Jordan: (sharpening pencil) I'm going to do this very sharp!

Stephen: Shut up, will you, Jordan!

Jordan: Shut up, you, you Pakistan!

Stephen: That's why Pakistan beat England! At cricket! Init? (to PC)

PC: What?

Stephen: Pakistan beat England at cricket?

PC: Yeah.

Stephen: (to Jordan) Ahhh! 'Cos I'm a Paki!

Jordan: (laughs)

Stephen: Init? I'm half-Paki and he's half-Paki!

PC: Are you?

Jordan: I'm half-Indian 'cos I'm a West Indian!

PC: You're a West Indian?

Jordan: I'm a little bit English and I come from Jamaica with my dad. Like this: chill out, man!

Stephen: I bet![31]

In this exchange, we see one child (Jordan) attempt to silence another (Stephen) by maliciously labeling him a "Pakistan." Unexpectedly, Stephen proudly reclaims this intended slur and recasts it as a compliment, noting the superb cricket play of the Pakistani team. Suddenly the term, intended as one of domination and exclusion, becomes enticing to several students who excitedly proclaim their linkage to Pakistan or other foreign countries.

I believe that students can be pushed to offer their own interpretations of controversial words and to investigate their histories in ways that both mimic and extend the efforts of Stephen. Such an activity can make students more sensitive to their own use or alteration of offensive speech. Even at very young ages, students can be introduced to these activities. I recently viewed a film, *It's Elementary*, which documents an early elementary class engaging in a discussion about a potentially controversial identity term. The teacher asked, "What does 'gay' mean?" Students offered an array of responses: "happy," "sick," "hugging," "love," and "biracial relationship." The teacher steered away from some extreme outliers and offered a broad definition of gay as same-sex love but largely allowed the students' definitions to stand. Students had the opportunity to challenge more hateful definitions themselves as well as to reissue "gay" with the meaning of some of the alternatives they listed. Such an activity could lead to mis- (possibly even better) appropriations of the term.

Butler's thoughts on reworking language are noteworthy because they show how the sense of agency and change emerging from her work differs from the account of habitus offered by Bourdieu. Butler argues that Bourdieu does not recognize the Derridean break of language where the ordinary language that brings a being into existence is ruptured by unexpected, extraordinary speech.[32] Butler locates the power of speech in this break rather than in the link between current language and prior context as Bourdieu does. This break is able to contest the sedimented ordinary. She highlights the capacity for speech to be used creatively or unexpectedly rather than emphasizing the tendency of Bourdieu's view of language as perpetuating the past.

Butler's notion of agency reveals and indirectly addresses some of the problems with Bourdieu's theory. For Butler, agency necessarily includes the ability to be innovative, whether through language, performance, or parody. One cannot be so if overly determined by the social field in which one is located. It appears that this is the case with the habitus. One becomes so fixed by lengthy exposure to cultural norms that, even while one can affect the world, one's historically sedimented ways of being prevent one from doing so in original or creative ways.

Additionally, Bourdieu claims that one must reside in a position of social power if one's utterances are to have force and effect. Butler's sense of agency via linguistic insurrection suggests that force and effect can issue from those not in a position of social power. This can occur through unexpected linguistic breaks, parodic performance, exploitation of official speech, or unexpectedly responding to interpellations of race and gender.[33] As I ex-

plain in the coming chapters, my notion of flexible habits adopts these linguistic acts of agency and innovation in order to show how the body can more
greatly impact identity transformation and change of social structures than the
concept of habitus allows. By showing that people from nondominant groups
can successfully disrupt problematic social norms through performatives, I
attribute the capacity for agency to those who lack social status. This prevents
the maintenance of the status quo (as that desired by those already occupying
dominant positions) and the denial of power to those who lack social status
as is the case in Bourdieu's work. We must be careful, however, not to suggest that those individuals of lower social status are not tasked with a duty to
perform insurrection. To solely place the burden of changing social systems
on the shoulders of those who have already suffered disproportionately would
not be just. We should, nonetheless, celebrate moments when such individuals invoke their agency and strive to create environments that welcome it.

Revealing the Performativity of Identity

I have already alluded to the final act of insurrection resulting from Butler's
depiction of subject formation: the use of parody and performance. She encourages subjects to perform their identities in ways that reveal the performativity of gender itself. Such efforts reveal that gender is not a static essence
but rather the effect of an activity that the body is compelled to repeat. Her
most famous example, drag, highlights the performative aspect of gender and
disrupts normative claims regarding the naturalness of gender.

THE ROLE OF SCHOOLS

Butler characterizes many of the insurrectionary acts she calls for as spontaneous, claiming that they occur by chance or without reflection or intent. In
many instances, she may be correct in this assessment. However, as my description of reworking language in the previous section shows, many of these
acts appear to require certain skills, knowledges, or propensities. In the reworking of racial slurs, for example, children are more effective when they
are able to skillfully time their language use, when they have knowledge of
the word's history, or when they are prone to inducing linguistic play with
words. If this is the case, as I think it is, schools as sites of social justice and
youth development should be tasked with developing these traits. Schools
that genuinely want to improve life's conditions by producing students capable of ameliorating problems of social hierarchy should be honing these
skills.

While protest can occur by chance, its effects are often fleeting and produced or noticed by only a select few. This leaves schools in a strange
predicament. On the one hand, if some outliers protest identity practices,
small change can be made, but larger goals are difficult to achieve. On the
other hand, if nearly every student protests without some sense of a shared
project or goal, change becomes disorganized and sets up an institution that
must penalize or prohibit certain acts so as to maintain a sense of order or purpose. When knowledge and skill sets relative to living and transforming one's
identity are cultivated in the classroom, the political agency and sensitivity of
each child is refined and linked with others in ways that increase the likelihood of long-lasting, widespread success. Moreover, targeting schools is particularly fitting for the aims of both Butler and Dewey, for both describe children as not yet fully set in their ways or sedimented into fully coherent and
distinct identities. Developmentally, the congealing of identity coincides with
schooling. Because children enter schools without well-established identities,
they are in a unique and powerful position. They have the ability to shape not
only the identity a child develops but also how he or she inhabits that identity
and handles social problems related to it.

The insubordinate political acts Butler describes are portrayed in highly
theoretical terms, often leaving the practical ways in which these acts would
play out difficult to detect. While I have provided some concrete examples
through references to actual classroom scenarios, I acknowledge that Butler's
esoteric description is both beneficial and detrimental. Butler rightly notes
that one cannot lay out ahead of time the criteria that determine which acts
count as insubordinate.[34] These criteria are contextually dependent and constantly changing as identity categories, as well as the words that describe
them, vary over time and location. Attempting to pin them down in concrete
examples offers only a limited picture of insurrection, one that may not be
valid when encountered by other readers in the future. Pinning down examples might also wrongly imply a definitive model for what or how to protest
identity problems. Butler is also correct in warning that implementing a specific mass countermovement would simply replace one normative way of being raced or gendered with another, without continually pushing the borders
of how people live their lives as members of identity categories.

Despite all this, Butler's abstract prose leaves the general public, including
teachers who are also concerned with alleviating the problems of hierarchies
and identity sedimentation, with little concrete direction for how they can cultivate students who can confront these problems and successfully rework notions of race and gender. In the next chapter, I fashion a platform for agency
out of a specific interpretation of Dewey's habits that is guided by a Butlerian notion of power, subjectivity, performativity, and political goals. By de-

scribing political change in terms of a way of educating that teachers already undertake—the development of habits rather than through an obscure language of discourse and the symbolic—I aim to offer a more robust sense of agency and identity transformation that is compatible with current teacher practice and palatable to teacher understanding. Before entering that discussion, however, allow me to bring together the views of both Dewey and Butler on subjectivity, embodiment, identity, and agency in the concluding half of this chapter.

DEWEY AS ILLUMINATED BY BUTLER

Butler's theory of subjectivity and embodiment clarifies and extends many of Dewey's more subtle points on the topic. Butler's analysis of language especially sheds light on Dewey's notions of transaction and the body as socially constructed activity. Butler's performativity shows a great deal of similarity to Dewey's habits but pushes farther to suggest directions for the possibility of change.

First, Butler's thesis on language as discursively constituting the embodied subject helps one better understand how Dewey's organism is constituted through transactions with the environment. She more explicitly delineates social norms, linguistic codes, and cultural laws as key factors influencing the transactive encounter. Thereby she lends more extensive analysis to Dewey's claim that "the meaning of native activities is not native, it is acquired. It depends upon interaction with a matured social medium."[35] Despite this statement, he often operates as though certain aspects of the body, typically impulses, are native and untouched by social forces.[36] Butler's more detailed account shows how the effects of language are thoroughgoing, making even some of the most simple bodily elements appear native or essential when they are actually socially constructed. Via Butler, then, the ways in which even apparently native activities necessarily entail social construction becomes more clear. Although Dewey's definition of "environment" entails a wide range of the organic and cultural, Butler provides a more in-depth account of the transactive elements of the environment, especially language, that influence social construction and are often lost in Dewey's sweeping use of the term.

Dewey claims that bodies do not have essences that they reflect. Butler, through her analysis of gender, however, pushes farther to explain how bodies may appear to display certain physiologically determined traits but actually are performing socially mandated ways of living that constitute us as linguistically and politically recognizable subjects. Butler helps us understand the normative elements that affect the ways we live our lives, how they depend on the cooperation of our bodies for their survival, and how they can be changed via our bodily plays on them. While Dewey is aware that cultural constructs divide us into discretely categorized groups, including gender and race, Butler explicitly labels these as normative and hierarchical. Furthermore, she goads us beyond Dewey's claims by illuminating pathways for dealing with or changing the seeming essences of bodily identity.

Dewey understands the body as activity. Driven by social melioration, Dewey wants us to look at the effects of embodied activities to decide whether they are satisfying, while Butler wants us to focus on what bodies actually do. She pushes past Dewey by showing that the activity is not done by a subject that preexists the deed. Drawing on Friedrich Nietzsche, Butler shows that the body does the deed male, courageous, and so on rather than *is* male, courageous, and the like.[37] The trait of male is assigned to the body because of the way it coherently enacts the social definition of male; the body is not male before it is signified as so. Read together, Butler and Dewey show that analyzing the actual doings of bodies and their effects can highlight whether the doings are satisfying and whether they should be continued. Looking at socially instituted performance sheds light on social norms and how they may form categorical hierarchies and other social problems.

Butler shows how seeming constraints on embodied living, like gender norms, can be productive and offer us avenues for resistance and social change. Because these constraints constitute us, she argues that we must work from within their bounds to achieve transformation. Her argument elucidates Dewey's understanding of structure. Sullivan explains, "Like the structure of a house, which is not something the house submits to but is what allows it to effectively be what it is, the cultural constructs that structure us *are* us."[38] The social constructs that constitute us are not laid on a neutral surface (the body) but rather are us, including our ability to change them. For Dewey, then, we cannot challenge the social configurations that are problematic for us from without because we rely on them for our very sense of self and our ability to affect the world.

Neither Butler nor Dewey sees the body as passive, but Butler, through her critique of Foucault, helps us to see that even while cultural norms are read onto the body, the body remains active in the way that it repeats those norms. Understanding this repetition in terms of habits illuminates Dewey's view of the body as active through transaction and plasticity of habit. Dewey notes,

> The organism acts in accordance with its own structure, simple or complex, upon its surroundings. As a consequence the changes produced in the environment react upon the organism and its activities. The living creature undergoes, suffers, the consequences of its own behavior.[39]

In this way, the embodied organism is active in effecting the ways it is constituted.

When addressing the active nature of bodies and the performance of identity, Butler adds,

> If gender is a kind of a doing, an incessant activity performed, in part, without one's knowing and without one's willing, it is not for that reason automatic or mechanical. On the contrary, it is a practice of improvisation within a scene of constraint. Moreover, one does not "do" one's gender alone. One is always "doing" with or for another, even if the other is only imaginary.[40]

This account particularly enhances and clarifies Dewey's notion of habit. Here we see how habit can feel and behave as though rote, unconscious repetition and yet not be *merely* mechanical, for it also entails opportunities for variation on those socially constrained activities. When parallels are drawn between the performativity of gender and the habits of identity that I am deducing from Dewey, this quote also reveals that habits are often wrongly connoted as property of individuals. Habits are actually social performances, enacted for, alongside, or by virtue of others. Others provide the enabling capacities of habits and the meaning-making audience that renders them efficacious.

For Dewey, habits give one efficacy in the world. They are the mechanisms that express will and are in direct contact with the organism's surroundings.[41] As I describe in greater detail in chapter 5, Dewey locates power in the ability to vary and acquire new habits.[42] Butler's theory of performativity, with all its similarity to Dewey's theory of plastic habits, extends Dewey's claim to show that efficacy is achieved by altering the way one customarily enacts his or her habits in ways that challenge or misrepresent the cultural influences affecting them. She urges us to misappropriate the typical ways in which we are problematically hailed to upset them, thereby disturbing their perceived stability and appropriateness—the way they appear natural and fixed on the body. Butler's performativity points toward directions for employing the flexibility of Dewey's organisms in socially and politically valuable ways. Importantly, given Dewey's concept of transaction, she shows how organisms can affect their social environments and vice versa not in a simple back-and-forth direction but rather in intricate, spiraling variations. Thus, Butler elucidates the complexity of Dewey's notion of transaction and extends his hope for the flexibility of habits in fruitful directions.

Both Butler and Dewey have a sense of the incompleteness of the body. Both see it as constantly changing and incapable of being fully grasped. Butler argues that this incompleteness leaves a space for contestation of identity

categories. She describes bodily excess, which is not pinned down in set social performatives and which exceeds interpellation but can trouble those performances, disrupting them and the norms they display. Thereby, Butler gives
explanation to the role of the impulses that Dewey names as not yet coalesced
into habits but of which he gives little other description as to their role or
transformative capacity.

Butler thinks Bourdieu does not understand the excess of the body. She
claims that Bourdieu portrays cultural institutions as stagnant and incapable
of being changed by individuals and by their bodily performatives in particular. Because Bourdieu assumes that constituting norms are fully effective in
their aims and constraints, Butler thinks he does not see moments where the
socially constructed body exceeds an interpellation and thereby contests it.[43]
Butler thinks Bourdieu does not acknowledge how bodily performativity can
confound the social fields that cultivate it rather than simply repeating or
resinscribing them. McNay adds that Bourdieu does not account for indeterminacy—how the body may not take on the norms it learns from culture exactly and therefore leaves a space for contestation of those norms.[44] I think
both of these are valid criticisms of Bourdieu. While Butler criticizes Bourdieu's habitus for being fully fixed and without excess, Dewey's impulses offer an unaffiliated alternative—bodily elements that have not yet been directed by social norms and are not yet fully intelligible.[45] These impulses
spark indeterminacies where the body is suddenly steered in new directions
and fails to precisely repeat its habitual activities of the past.

A final way in which Butler's theory illuminates that of Dewey is in terms
of social control and freedom. In *Experience and Education*, Dewey talks at
length about self-control and distinguishes positive from negative freedom.
Dewey wants children to learn self-control by reflecting on the consequences
of their bodily actions. Such reflection allows the student to make meaning of
their position in the world and their effects on it. While not calling for control, Butler directs attention to reflecting on one's bodily activity in ways that
encourage alteration when pigeonholed into problematic identities and social
positions. Both thinkers appreciate physical self-awareness, though Butler extends her appreciation in the direction of social and political change, while
Dewey's tends to be more aligned with achieving one's needs and improving
daily communal living.

For Dewey, negative freedom is freedom from restriction. However, he acknowledges that the organism can never be entirely free from the social conditions that constitute it. It can, nonetheless, acquire the positive freedom to
frame purposes, to carry out intentions, and to change its way of living within
those conditions viewed as enabling. Dewey values positive freedom because
he understands that we must work within the structures that constitute us in

order to change them.[46] Butler also recognizes the restriction that comes from stagnant social hierarchies affecting embodied experience. She wants to work toward a positive freedom to remake oneself in new and different ways. While Dewey understands positive freedom as the liberty to frame purposes that arise from intelligent reflection on bodily impulses and objective conditions,[47] Butler pushes this into the freedom to redefine one's very embodied self via objective conditions. Together, they point toward habits and performativity as the avenue for enacting such freedom.

CHALLENGING DEWEY

While Butler's theory of embodiment illuminates and extends Dewey's theory in many important ways, it also contradicts Dewey's in others. Most of their differences revolve around Dewey's efforts to maintain bodily stability and stasis and Butler's attempts to radically change and possibly dissolve identity.

Earlier I explained how both thinkers envision the body as permeable. Butler extends her discussion of permeability in a new direction by exploring how alternative sexual practices alter the boundaries of the body. In *Gender Trouble*, she notes,

> The construction of stable bodily contours relies upon fixed sites of corporeal permeability and impermeability. Those sexual practices in both homosexual and heterosexual contexts that open surfaces and orifices to erotic signification or close down others effectively reinscribe the boundaries of the body along new cultural lines.[48]

In this way, Butler shows that the permeability of the body through a transactive encounter can allow the body to morph into something new, bearing new meaning and signification. While Dewey is open to the need and possibility for change, especially in terms of blurring bodily distinction, he also largely desires stability. He describes humans as needing to maintain stasis in order for them to survive, learn, interact, and take pleasure in their lives. Butler, however, shows that maintaining a stable bodily exterior and established customs for sexual transaction preserves the status quo of acceptable bodying and actually firms up bodily separation. She locates the surface of the body as a place of political contestation and subversion rather than stability.

While Dewey values stability, he largely appreciates the plasticity of habits. Dewey thinks the plasticity of our habits allows us to vary our styles of being until we locate "appropriate and efficient ways of acting."[49] While Butler would applaud Dewey's desire to maintain the unpredictable variation of habits, she would disapprove of his desire to change habits so that one can live most efficiently. For Butler, these criteria can be key markers of enforced hierarchy and inequality. For a white man, for example, to locate the most appropriate and efficient ways of acting, he may be led to adopting certain practices of racial or gender discrimination that maintain his privileged role in the world. Such practices allow him to continue his life with ease. Popular racist or sexist worldviews prevent him from seeing these acts as inappropriate because he may not hold an adequate ethical schema for considering the effects of his acts on minorities. As I suggest in the next chapter, Dewey may actually have a more just and democratic sense of "appropriate and efficient." Reading Butler's critique of Bourdieu onto Dewey, she is discontent with the suggestion that change of habit is motivated by environmental necessity.[50] For, in her view, it may never appear necessary to alter certain systems of hierarchy, thus leaving stagnant and unjust habits intact. Because of this, performativity is not narrowly sparked by environmental necessity or the desire for balance.

Butler further complicates the gendered status quo by referencing mind–body dualism. While Dewey is leery of this binary, he does not expose it, as Butler does, for its gendered parallels. Man is positively associated with the mind and woman negatively with the body.[51] Butler, in fact, focuses extensively on rigid categories of identity that set up binaries and hierarchies. While both theorists want to alleviate the rigidity of categories of embodied being that currently dictate how we live, Butler takes this a step farther than Dewey is willing to go. It appears that Butler may want to get rid of categories of identity entirely. Categories, for Butler, must be interpreted and assigned meaning, an act that necessarily entails exclusion and thereby limits acceptable ways of living in reference to some criteria. Dewey values these categories of identity to some degree because they guide us in enacting our freedom and pursuing our interests; they teach us about ourselves and options available to us. Indeed, he calls for learning situations that target our identities and further their expression.[52] While Butler pushes us to see identity categories as normative causes of hierarchies and social problems, Dewey is far more comfortable with maintaining them. In order to achieve agency, Butler insists that we need to forgo our efforts to maintain stable categories of self-identity and be willing to be interpellated within and outside the categories in which we used to envision ourselves so that we may subversively misrecognize and misrepresent them.[53]

DEWEY AND BUTLER TOGETHER ON AGENCY

Butler and Dewey offer useful and provocative notions of agency. Both, however, have shortcomings and inconsistencies. This section investigates some of those problems and considers how, when read together, each theory may help rescue the other from certain pitfalls. I conclude the section by showing how these concerns and possible solutions might help craft a more robust vision of agency that does not arise from mere passive subjectification but rather entails dynamic self-transformation and a deep sense of self. This account of agency overcomes not only shortcomings in Dewey and Butler's work but also criticisms waged against both linguistically unsophisticated theories and poststructural theories that undertheroize embodied experience. Unlike some feminist and poststructural scholars, I conceive of agency in terms other than domination/resistance or signification/resignification by keeping centered in the material relations and the social complexities of schools where habits are formed and changed.[54] This allows for my account of agency to invoke a platform for change that neither repeats past forms of domination nor overlooks structural constraints to unbridled resignification.

First, Butler's criticisms of Bourdieu's habitus can inform Dewey's notion of habit spelled out here. Habitus and Dewey's habits bear significant resemblance but differ considerably given Dewey's depiction of transaction. Butler argues that Bourdieu focuses too much on how the habitus is formed than on how it or the environment can be changed.[55] She charges him with a more structuralist reading of social institutions as determining the construction of the subject once and for all, therefore eliminating a space for agency and significant change.[56] While Dewey's habits are also largely constructed by present cultural forces, they are not determined. Rather, transaction is a continuous process of subject formation, undergoing continual change. It is not prompted by a stimulus but rather is always actively engaging with the world around it and the subject's present habits. The process extends in both directions — as the subject is formed and changed, alteration of exterior conditions occurs. Moreover, change of the environment can be specifically targeted when change of habit occurs at the level of intelligent reflection, taking environmental problems into consideration.

Butler contends that in the moments when Bourdieu does describe change of habitus, it is motivated by environmental necessity. In many instances, change of habit for Dewey is also provoked by changes in the world that demand the subject's adaptation in order to maintain stability. Butler argues that it may never appear necessary to alter certain systems of oppression or hierarchy, thus leaving stagnant and unjust habits intact. Butler claims that iterability is not narrowly sparked by environmental necessity or the desire for balance. Rather, it typically occurs spontaneously or within the movement of language itself. I largely agree with Butler's criticism that change should not be simply sparked by environmental conditions, but I also think that nearly the same critique could be leveled at Butler.[57] For it is not clear in her account why subjects would be motivated to change the discursive power structures that constitute them, particularly if they maintain a space of privilege for that subject. From the example of the British school divided into black/white and South Asian, for example, it seems unlikely that the white boys would be motivated to change or forgo the privileged space carved out for them on the playground. It is a space that brings them pleasure and that they work hard to maintain. Because of these concerns, dealing with unjust habits is a problem of education. Within school walls, teachers can craft situations that reveal problems such as white privilege that might otherwise go unnoted or unchallenged by students. Those teachers can also cultivate a standard of assessing equality and identity issues as students judge the success of their actions, thereby highlighting moments and issues in need of alteration and provoking students to engage them. Change of habit, of the performance of identity, and of the social institutions that support them, then, is neither narrowly the result of environmental necessity nor linguistic happenstance.

Butler is correct, however, in drawing attention to the play and failures of language, for it is there that she identifies a key element missing from Dewey's account of agency and change. It is fair to say that Butler would also apply her criticism of Bourdieu's inability to recognize the break of language onto Dewey.[58] Dewey, too, does not see that the ordinary language that brings us into being can be ruptured by an unexpected, extraordinary speech act. Butler, drawing on Jacques Derrida, locates the power of speech in this break, which forcefully interrupts linguistic tradition by introducing the unspeakable out of context, rather than in the linking of language to prior context, as is the case with Bourdieu. This break is able to contest the sedimented ordinary and is the back on which agency rides. While Dewey certainly includes language within his more encompassing term "environment," he underestimates its potential as a platform for agency, and a more nuanced notion of agency must centrally draw on this potential.

Problems arise, however, when the play of language seems to exclude an active agent, and this is a fault of Butler's theory. As was described earlier, the subject must engage in citation to continue to exist, and agency is located within moments of resignification—moments that often occur by chance. Veronica Vasterling has persuasively argued that because the reiteration takes place in the movement of language itself, agents really have limited intention over it.[59] She rightly contends that the resulting notion of agency is not very viable insofar as the subject is not much of an active participant in the shaping of its own existence, the content, and the way it cites. Butler fails to show how subjects can actively rework the circumstances in which they find themselves via iteration. A closer reading of Butler does reveal that just because we cannot ensure that our words will be received in the ways we intend does not mean that we cannot act intentionally. Rather, we can try to steer resigni-

fication and the production of certain types of meaning, including the exposure of exclusion I described earlier. Vasterling astutely responds that this can
be legitimate agency because it has initiative and intervention but adds that it
must be picked up by others to effect broad change. Dewey's transactional account that poses a closer linking of people and educational situations where
students work together to achieve desired ends can provide the social aspects
and provocation of initiative that makes the more active sense of agency
Vasterling seeks complete.

Indeed habit, for Dewey, is inherently social. This differs considerably
from Butler's more individualistic account of performativity and iterability.
Butler theorizes the agency of the individual and, while accounting for others
as the audience of performatives, undertheorizes collective social action. For
Dewey, habits are never divorced from associated living and with working toward improving living conditions with others. Dewey depicts freedom as intelligent use of habits and the impulses they organize, where intelligence is
geared toward growth and social flourishing. Political agency still begins
with the individual but is necessarily and intricately connected to others via
transaction. Dewey's notion of political agency is inseparable from living the
democratic life. Butler's portrait of linguistic construction, on the other hand,
implicates other people but is not reciprocal. Butler's account does not show
how the political protests of the individual are connected to those of others or
their well-being.

Bodily habit, via transaction, is always constituted by influences from
without that interact with impulses and inquiry, then necessarily extend back
outward to interact with the cultural environment. This sets the stage for corporeal enactments that confound the structures that compel and constrain
them and often do so publicly and alongside others. While also allowing a
space for discursive acts of resistance, Dewey's habit pushes past Butler's ad-
herence to linguistic insurrection. Furthermore, Dewey offers a way of understanding the concrete realities of living bodies, including the corporeal experiences of material inequalities and their potential for corporeal resistance.
Although Butler asserts that language can have real effects on bodies, habits
both display and protest those effects, thereby offering a more complete sense
of agency.[60]

Educational ethnographer Paul Connolly shares a telling example. He remarks that one black girl, Annette, was a skilled sports player who used her
classroom disruptiveness and athletic ability to establish herself as one of the
boys. She came to be respected by the other boys, who admired the ways she
habitually stood up to the physical and verbal attacks of a bullying boy. She
eventually achieved a position of dominance in their group, especially on the
playground, where she had a commanding presence on the playing field and

determined which boys could join the game and which could not. Her leading position, however, was jeopardized one day when the boys were proudly reporting that Annette had broken off another girl's coat peg. As she and her friends gloat, she sits down next to Paul, thereby upsetting Daniel, who wanted Annette to sit by him and who felt as though his position in the group had been taken. Daniel taunts Annette, proclaiming that Paul pinches Annette's bum and is going to have sex with her.[61] In this instance, we see that Annette works against the feminized and sexualized language typically used to describe girls through her athletic competence, her brave stance in the face of male aggressors, and her tendency to be disruptive in the classroom. Other classmates witness these corporeal acts of resistance, and many note them with awe and respect. And while perhaps some begin to envision new possibilities for gender because of her acts, Daniel attempts to maintain traditional gender roles by reinterpellating Annette as a sex object.

Two related critiques have been waged against Butler's oversight of the corporeal aspects of agency. Lois McNay argues that Butler does not give an account of the felt, lived experience of gender as performative. McNay claims that this makes Butler's notion of agency seem devoid of actual human experience and social or historical location.[62] Because habits are the most essential aspects of the everyday activities of each individual, they necessarily bear with them that individual's particularity, the conditions of his or her context, and his or her vested interest in the experience of gender and oppression. Nancy Fraser has also argued that Butler does not account for embodied intersubjectivity. I believe that when habits are understood in the context of everyday associated living with others, the goals of democracy, and the process of transaction, a more complete picture of embodied intersubjectivity appears.

Fraser, Nussbaum, and similar critics who have faulted Butler's theory because of its individualism and focus on politics through language have also raised concerns with the lack of criteria for determining which of the variations of identities and political formations Butler describes are good. Fraser faults Butler for valorizing resignification as being good simply by virtue of being change and not providing criteria for what counts as good change. Neither agency nor the ability to resist ensure political effectiveness, and Butler does not show us how to analyze the effects acts of resistance do have.

Fraser in *Justice Interruptus* and in her exchange with three other feminists, including Butler, in *Feminist Contentions* takes issue not only with Butler's antihumanist portrait of politics as language and impersonal signification but also with Butler's valorization of resignification. She worries that resignification does not necessarily entail any positive change, nor does it provide a criterion for assessing the success of any change that does occur.

She asks, "Can't there be bad (oppressive, reactionary) resignifications? In opting for the epistemically neutral 'resignification,' as opposed to the epistemically positive 'critique,' Butler seems to valorize change for its own sake and thereby to disempower feminist judgment."[63] To this insightful question, Butler rather unsatisfactorily replies,

> My question is not whether certain kinds of significations are good or bad, warranted or unwarranted, but, rather: what constitutes the domain of discursive possibility within which and about which such questions can be posed? My argument is that "critique," to use Fraser's terms, always takes place *immanent* to the regime of discourse/power whose claims it seeks to adjudicate, which is to say that the practice of "critique" is implicated in the very power-relations it seeks to adjudicate. There is no pure place outside of power by which the question of validity might be raised, and where validity is raised, it is also always an activity of power.[64]

While Butler rightly notes the importance of focusing on the domain of possibility, especially because extending possibilities is a necessity to those who are outside linguistic acceptability,[65] her response is unsatisfactory for several reasons. First, her claim that critique or any other form of epistemic normativity is always wrapped up in the power relations it investigates is a truism with little to offer. Of course, systems of warrant are themselves implicated in power. This does not mean that they cannot be used beneficially or at least strategically in specific contexts. Second, Fraser is right to suggest that *feminist* judgment and other types of normative or politically motivated assessment are jeopardized by focusing on unbounded resignification. Those people interested in ensuring the well-being of oppressed groups are largely stripped of their assessment tools and left unable to determine which living conditions are better or worse. Instead, they can only label variations as different. Moreover, under Butler's scheme, these activists are unable to shape a vision for better living to guide their work; rather, they can only uphold change and possibility.

In much the same spirit, though with a far sharper tongue, Nussbaum raises a similar concern with Butler. She faults Butler for not upholding a normative vision that can guide and access political change. She claims that Butler does not differentiate good subversions that confront problems with identity and bad subversions that work against justice. Nussbaum fervently argues that norms like equality must be articulated in order to lead successful or even worthy political protest.

Both Fraser and Nussbaum offer valid criticisms of Butler, especially in her early works. More recently, Butler has conceded to some of their criticisms but still wants to focus on the realm of possibility rather than discretely defining which possibilities are good or bad. Nonetheless, she ends her most recent book with a noteworthy concession that I quote at length:

> Which action is right to pursue, which innovation has value, and which does not? The norms that we would consult to answer this question cannot themselves be derived from resignification. They have to be derived from a radical democratic theory and practice; thus, resignification has to be contextualized in that way. One must make substantive decisions about what will be a less violent future, what will be a more inclusive population, what will help to fulfill, in substantive terms, the claims of universality and justice that we seek to understand in their cultural specificity and social meaning. When we come to deciding right and wrong courses of action in that context, it is crucial to ask: what forms of community have been created, and through what violences and exclusions have they been created?[66]

Here we see Butler allowing that assessments of present states of living can and should be derived from norms of radical democratic theory. Importantly, Butler still rightly refuses to define these norms in terms of content. Rather, she depicts their properties by saying that they should be owned or wielded by no person in particular, they should not coerce identities into normalized positions, and, most notably, they should establish collective ties between people founded on political activism.[67] Noticeably astonished at this recent development in her own claims, Butler says, "So I have concluded it seems with a call to extend the norms that sustain viable life."[68] Her shift from overthrowing normative claims is surprising but admirable.

As I detail further in chapter 5, when Dewey is read in contrast to Butler, pragmatism can offer a justification for which reworkings of habit and which instances of political change are good, though Dewey still recognizes, as Butler warns, that these criteria themselves are already wrapped up in power. While Dewey would dissuade holding a comprehensive portrait of the good life for the future, the pragmatist notions of truth and flourishing can provide judgment on the goodness and effectiveness of acts as well as point toward directions for future change. Moreover, when these pragmatist principles are seated within the political ideals of democracy, criteria of equality, justice, and associated living may be drawn on. While Nussbaum, however, thinks that norms like equality need to be fully articulated, a Deweyan reading of co-ordinated habit would suggest that these visions do not have to be fully articulated. Instead, if their elements are experienced at the level of satisfactory embodied living, they will be sought and maintained. Furthermore, if those aspects are foregrounded, identity change entails the critical component that distinguishes it from willy-nilly identity "border crossing" or simple celebration of flexibility, as problematically supported by some multicultural educators and other postmodern queer theorists.[69]

A ground-level criterion that Dewey would uphold is that of constructive communication. As opposed to Butler's linguistic disjoint, which certainly can be fruitful in itself, habits seek to lead us through successful interaction, including communication. Butler's variations on repetition, however, reach a moment of impasse where a problem with the world has been revealed but not resolved. Restored communication for Dewey is restored coordinated action—action that can work to improve the well-being of all parties involved and therefore extends political agency to the acts of a group. Communication is not only a criterion of successful acts of political agency but also a tool for fostering them. Insofar as changing one's self relies on or is aided by the observations of others who communicate problems they notice with that person's habits back to him or her, political change becomes a more social process, a process of communication and education. Teachers and students can engage in these types of discussions by acutely watching the habitual activity of other students and sharing their remarks on problems or injustices that those habits present so that they become fodder for inquiry and change.

When taken together, their theories of agency show valuable points of overlap and supplement one another in areas of weakness. Both locate agency within the process of subject construction and offer similar accounts of how it is carried out through performativity and habit. Combining Butler's sophisticated account of power, appreciation for linguistic insubordination, and focus on problems of identity coherence with Dewey's embodied notion of habits, the ongoing process of transaction, and pragmatist and democratic criteria for political effectiveness offers a more robust notion of political agency that I sum up under the Deweyan-inspired name of flexible habits. The next chapter depicts flexible habits and their process of change in greater detail.

NOTES

1. Bronwyn Davies, quoting Rebecca Kantor, in "The Discursive Production of the Male/Female Dualism in School Settings," in *The RoutledgeFalmer Reader in Sociology of Education*, ed. Stephen J. Ball (London: RoutledgeFalmer, 2004), 135–36.

2. Judith Butler, "Sex and Gender in Simone de Beauvoir's *Second Sex*," *Yale French Studies* 72 (1986): 45.

3. Judith Butler, *Gender Trouble: Tenth Anniversary Edition* (New York: Routledge, 1999), 130.

4. Judith Butler, *Excitable Speech: A Politics of the Performative* (New York: Routledge, 1997), 133.

5. Butler, *Excitable Speech* 135; Judith Butler, *Bodies That Matter: On the Discursive Limits of "Sex"* (New York: Routledge, 1993), 9.

6. Butler, *Gender Trouble*, xv.

7. Certainly, I am not suggesting that this young child overtly carries out this detailed thought process. I do, however, believe even children this young have a strong sense of the importance of gender (and ultimately linguistic) recognition and will work hard to achieve and maintain their status. I provide here an interpretation of those efforts.

8. Butler, *Bodies That Matter*, x.

9. Butler, *Gender Trouble*, 42 (italics in original).

10. Butler, *Bodies That Matter*, 7.

11. Butler, *Gender Trouble*, 144 (italics in original).

12. Mica Pollock, *Colormute: Race Talk Dilemmas in an American School* (Princeton, N.J.: Princeton University Press, 2004), 24.

13. Butler, *Bodies That Matter*, 93.

14. Butler, *Bodies That Matter*, 226–27.

15. Butler, *Bodies That Matter*; Butler, *Excitable Speech*, 51.

16. Butler, *Gender Trouble*, xiii.

17. Here the language is tricky, for they cannot exist as linguistic subjects if they do not fulfill cultural standards.

18. Butler, *Gender Trouble*, 22–23 (italics in original).

19. Gail Masuchika Boldt, "Sexist and Heterosexist Responses to Gender Bending in an Elementary Classroom," *Curriculum Inquiry* 26, no. 2 (1996): 117 (italics in original).

20. Debra Van Ausdale and Joe R. Feagin, *The First R: How Children Learn Race and Racism* (Lanham, Md.: Rowman & Littlefield, 2001), 37.

21. I am referring here to the work of Vivian Gussin Paley, which has been adopted by many practicing teachers, *You Can't Say You Can't Play* (Cambridge, Mass.: Harvard University Press, 1992).

22. Butler, *Bodies That Matter*, 122.

23. Here, again, the language of using "people" is tricky and not exactly accurate.

24. Judith Butler, *Undoing Gender* (New York: Routledge, 2004), 60–64.

25. Butler, *Undoing Gender*, 3–4.

26. Butler, *Undoing Gender*, 29.

27. Pollock, *Colormute*, 49.

28. Robert Alan Brookey and Diane Helene Miller, "Changing Signs: The Political Pragmatism of Poststructuralism," *International Journal of Sexuality and Gender Studies* 6, nos. 1–2 (2001): 142.

29. Butler, *Bodies That Matter*, 116–17.

30. Butler, *Excitable Speech*, 38.

31. Paul Connolly, *Racism, Gender Identities, and Young Children* (London: Routledge, 1998), 110.

32. Butler, *Excitable Speech*, 142–45.

33. Butler, *Excitable Speech*, 156.

34. Butler, *Gender Trouble*, xxi.

35. John Dewey, *Human Nature and Conduct* (1922; reprint, Mineola, N.Y.: Dover, 2002), 65.

36. Dewey, *Human Nature and Conduct*, 96.

37. Butler, *Gender Trouble*, 25.

38. Shannon Sullivan, "Reconfiguring Gender with John Dewey," *Hypatia* 15, no. 1 (2000): 26.

39. John Dewey, *Reconstruction in Philosophy* (1920; reprint, Boston: Beacon Press, 1957), 86.

40. Butler, *Undoing Gender*, 1.

41. Dewey, *Human Nature and Conduct*, 21.

42. John Dewey, *Experience and Nature* (Chicago: Open Court, 1925), 281.

43. Butler, *Excitable Speech*, 155.

44. Lois McNay, "Subject, Psyche, and Agency: The Work of Judith Butler," *Theory, Culture, and Society* 16, no. 2 (1999): 182.

45. Butler, *Excitable Speech*, 155. For more on this line of thinking, see Shannon Sullivan, *Living across and through Skins: Transactional Bodies, Pragmatism, and Feminism* (Bloomington: Indiana University Press, 2001), 100.

46. John Dewey, *Experience and Education* (Indianapolis: Kappa Delta Pi, 1998), 74.

47. Dewey, *Experience and Education*, 78.

48. Butler, *Gender Trouble*, 132.

49. John Dewey, *Democracy and Education* (New York: Free Press, 1916), 49.

50. Butler, *Excitable Speech*, 154.

51. Butler, *Gender Trouble*, 12.

52. John Dewey, *Outlines of a Critical Theory of Ethics*, in *The Early Works of John Dewey*, vol. 3, ed. Jo Ann Boydston (1891; reprint, Carbondale: Southern Illinois University Press, 1969), 305. Ana M. Martínez Alemán further explains Dewey's education as targeted on individual identities in "Identity, Feminist Teaching, and John Dewey," in *Feminist Interpretations of John Dewey*, ed. Charlene Haddock Seigfried (University Park: Pennsylvania State University Press, 2002), 120.

53. For more along these lines, see Sara Salih, *Judith Butler* (London: Routledge, 2002), 135.

54. Lois McNay notes the need for such an account of agency in *Gender and Agency: Reconfiguring the Subject in Feminist and Social Theory* (Malden, Mass.: Blackwell, 2000), 51 and 155.

55. Butler, *Excitable Speech*, 155–56.

56. Butler, *Bodies That Matter*, 9.

57. Indeed, Veronica Vasterling has issued such a critique in "Butler's Sophisticated Constructivism: A Critical Assessment," *Hypatia* 14, no. 3 (1999): 31.

58. Butler, *Excitable Speech*, 142.

59. Vasterling, "Butler's Sophisticated Constructivism," 28.

60. Butler, *Gender Trouble*, 148.

61. Connolly, *Gender Identities and Young Children*, 161.

62. McNay, "Subject, Psyche, and Agency," 178.

63. Fraser, *Justice Interruptus: Critical Reflections on the "Postsocialist" Condition* (New York: Routledge, 1997), 215.

64. Judith Butler, "For a Careful Reading," in *Feminist Contentions: A Philosophical Exchange*, ed. Seyla Benhabib, Judith Butler, Drucilla Cornell, and Nancy Fraser (New York: Routledge, 1995), 138–39.

65. Butler, *Undoing Gender*, 31.

66. Butler, *Undoing Gender*, 224–25.

67. Butler, *Undoing Gender*, 231.

68. Butler, *Undoing Gender*, 225.

69. For examples of these problematic suggestions, see Joe L. Kincheloe and Shirley R. Steinberg, "Addressing the Crisis of Whiteness," in *White Reign: Deploying Whiteness in America*, ed. Joe Kincheloe (New York: St. Martin's Griffin, 1998), 25, and Judith Halberstam, *In a Queer Time and Place* (New York: New York University Press, 2005), 18.

Chapter Five

Flexible Habits of Race and Gender

One spring, Renee, a young white girl, is comparing the color of her arms with another white child and a black/white biracial child. When she realizes that her arm is darker than the other girls' and that it has been getting increasingly darker, she asks her teacher if the change means she is no longer white. The teacher's aide laughs and tells her she is just getting a tan, not changing race. Renee frowns and looks unconvinced. Renee continues to be plagued by these thoughts and shares them with a black friend a few weeks later. Months pass, and she continues to contemplate the color of her skin and her racial identity. She told her mother that she wanted to be black and believed that the continued change in her skin color suggested that she could. When her mother said that was not possible, Renee grew very angry.[1] This interesting event depicts a child grappling with understanding the permanence of race—wondering how race changes, growing frustrated by adults who do not understand, and longing for the change to be complete. While Renee shows a superficial understanding of race, her ongoing wonder relates to this chapter's discussion of flexible habits and the ways in which they change our experience of race and racism.

In this chapter, I show how my understanding of these habits in terms of race and gender grows out of Dewey's work on habit in *Human Nature and Conduct* while it also challenges the brief and rare comments he makes on racism elsewhere. My depiction of flexible habits begins with Dewey's theory of habits but is guided by the account of performativity offered by Butler and the acts of political insurrection that follow from her theory of subjectivity. I show how Dewey himself hints at this understanding of habit through detailing his depiction of habit formation and change. While I briefly describe the role of schools in fostering flexible habits, I devote the final chapter to detailing how schools can and should cultivate flexible habits in students by analyzing classroom examples and envisioning alternative ways in which some of them might have played out.

RACIAL PREJUDICE

One of the few instances in which Dewey overtly discusses race and racism is in his essay "Racial Prejudice and Friction." There, Dewey describes racial prejudice, like any other prejudice, as an inkling that influences our judgments and actions:

> In other words, a prejudice is something which comes before judgment and prevents it or cuts it short; it is a desire or emotion which makes us see things in a particular light and gives a slant to all our beliefs.[2]

Prejudices entail our partialities toward or against certain objects or ways of being. These prejudices both originate from and play out at the level of habits. They can be the habitual ways in which we interact with and thereby make sense of the world around us. As habits, prejudices often do not operate at the level of conscious thought, though they certainly impact our formation of thoughts and judgments. For example, in not so many words, it was recently pointed out to me that I am biased against the color orange.[3] When shopping for clothing, my eyes gaze quickly over racks of orange sweaters, and I typically rush past them. This prejudice impacts my bodily habits and proclivities and likely influences my judgments about people dressed in orange or the beautiful outfits I envision myself wearing. One can see how similar prejudices regarding certain genders or races might behave likewise. They might steer us toward or away from certain groups or may lead us to certain assumptions about the group's members.

Racial prejudices often play out on our bodies in the ways we move, the expressions we make, and the ways we behave. Consider the prejudice conveyed by the woman in the fur coat in the rather lengthy though telling story that feminist scholar and poet Audre Lorde shares of being a young black girl on a Harlem train:

> I clutch my mother's sleeve, her arms full of shopping bags, Christmas-heavy. The wet smell of winter cloths, the train's lurching. My mother spots an almost seat, pushes my little snowsuited body down. On one side of me a man reading a paper. On the other, a woman in a fur hat staring at me. Her mouth twitches as she stares and then her gaze drops down, pulling mine with it. Her leather-gloved hand plucks at the line where my new blue snowpants and her sleek fur

coat meet. She jerks her coat closer to her. I look. I do not see whatever terrible thing she is seeing on the seat between us—probably a roach. But she has communicated her horror to me. It must be something very bad from the way she's looking, so I pull my snowsuit closer to me away from it, too. When I look up the woman is still staring at me, her nose holes and eyes huge. And suddenly I realize there is nothing crawling up the seat between us; it is me she doesn't want her coat to touch. The fur brushes past my face as she stands with a shudder and holds on to a strap in the speeding train. Born and bred a New York City child, I quickly slide over to make room for my mother to sit down. No word has been spoken. I'm afraid to say something to my mother because I don't know what I've done. I look at the sides of my snowpants, secretly. Is there something on them? Something's going on here I do not understand, but I will never forget it. Her eyes. The flared nostrils. The hate.[4]

No words or opinions are exchanged, yet the woman's prejudices are displayed through her body.

Dewey describes racial prejudice in particular as "the instinctive aversion of mankind to what is new and unusual, to whatever is different from what we are used to, and which thus shocks our customary habits."[5] Importantly, it is not that the new person is foreign to our home community (though this is sometimes the case), but it is by virtue of our habits "of thinking, of feeling, of talking, or observing and expecting that the new comer is foreign."[6] While it would seem that we make judgments about what is foreign, Dewey suggests that the sense of foreignness is relative to our own habits of "language, dress, manners."[7] These habits of our own become prejudices as they impact our judgments about the worth of different people. We assess others relative to our everyday customs. Aversion and its corresponding judgments about the inferiority of other peoples become caustic when it is manifested in coordination with the social and political power of a majority group against the person or group who is different. Dewey describes the resulting belief systems of group superiority as "racial friction." When this friction becomes widespread and systemic because it is carried out through the social and political power of the dominant group, we would recognize it today as racism.

Dewey poses a problematic solution to racial prejudice and friction. By describing aversion as "instinctive," he couches his discussion of racial prejudice in terms that make it appear natural and normal and thereby acceptable or defensible. He suggests that, after successful and prolonged exposure to the foreign, our habits come to terms with those different from us, and we no longer experience aversion. It would seem, then, that a contemporary approach to alleviating racism would be an intense and thoroughgoing intermixing of races for a considerable amount of time.[8] Indeed, many champions of school desegregation during the civil rights era as well as some more recent proponents of multicultural education have argued for their causes on similar grounds. Certainly there does seem to be some legitimacy to this view, and I am sure that there are many instances in which such mingling has been effective in reducing biased beliefs against races different from one's own. Often, however, such efforts underestimate the far-reaching impact of racial prejudice—the very embodied experiences of race that I have argued arise from Dewey's own account of habit elsewhere. Moreover, they are often guided by problematic assimilationist goals that undermine the value of the new or different race and jeopardize its ability to remain culturally strong. Indeed, in the essay "Racial Prejudice and Friction," Dewey's own depiction of racial prejudice and its alleviation suggests that habits try to domesticate the foreign and incorporate it into one's preexisting set of habits.

Contra Dewey's portrayal of assuaging racial prejudice, I do not think that our habits need to become familiar with those who are different from us in ways that transform (or conform) these newcomers into our present ways of being. Rather, I want to suggest that the habits themselves should be so flexible that they change—thereby changing our entire beings—when we engage with the new or different. Habits must not necessarily be hostile or even leery of the novel as Dewey seems to imply in this essay.[9] His suggestions here contradict the more nuanced and, I believe, accurate account of habit formation and change in his more lengthy works. There he explains how habits can confront and transform alongside newness with intrigue and excitement. As I show in this chapter, Dewey's theory in *Human Nature and Conduct* can be carefully extended in light of Butler's work to show that habits, when understood as flexible, can engage with other races in ways that are not hostile and in ways that do not propagate beliefs that they rightfully or naturally should be.

INQUIRY AND CHANGE OF HABIT

The sense of habits as flexible arises in part from Dewey's depiction of changing habits. Such change occurs through intelligent inquiry ignited by situations of conflict, impasse, or frustration. When our habits conflict or when they fail to keep up with the changing world, we may find ourselves uncomfortable, distracted, distraught, or unsure how to proceed. These conflicts disrupt the mechanization of habit that keeps us running smoothly. Dewey labels this event an "indeterminate situation."

Let's consider an example from the Disney movie *Remember the Titans* (2000). Early in the movie, the black and white football players of a newly desegregated high school meet for the first time. The scene is marked by white boys, walking stiffly, chests puffed, chins out, in a dominating mass met by the penetrating stares of black boys standing defensively, looking both frightened and angry. Smirks are exchanged and a few words are uttered, but only those that are perceived as insults are acknowledged. A short while later, the black teammates are gathered in the gymnasium for a meeting, when a chubby, jovial white boy comes bounding into the room, arms bouncing leisurely at his side. Without even thinking, he introduces himself as a new student, Louie, a navy kid freshly transplanted to Virginia. He shouts out a friendly hello through a cheeky smile and turns to make eye contact and wave to the crowd of black guys around him. The other guys, accustomed to racial tension and friendships divided by the color line, stand flabbergasted and unsure how to respond.

In this instance we see that an indeterminate situation arises when the black boys' typical ways of confronting their white counterparts are met by unexpected friendliness. The boys' habitual ways of acting are suddenly awkward, ineffective, or inappropriate. We see in their change of stance and countenance that they are caught off guard and momentarily paralyzed. They become frozen when they are unable to quickly adapt to the new boy and when their habits of cross-racial interaction and past experiences with racism conflict with their habitual responses to someone who is open and friendly. This experience of an indeterminate situation is guttural, corporeal—it is felt in one's posture and in one's level of comfort.

When the situation rises to the level of consciousness, when one realizes that something is awry and must be addressed, Dewey claims the situation becomes "problematic." It is at this point that inquiry begins. For Dewey, "*Inquiry is the controlled or directed transformation of an indeterminate situation into one that is so determinate in its constituent distinctions and relations as to convert the elements of the original situation into a unified whole.*"[10] Unlike more popular understandings of inquiry as simply a mental escapade, Dewey's definition of inquiry entails a component of intelligent reflection, an aspect of bodily change, and, importantly, a transformation of the situation, including both the objective conditions and the transaction between the organism and its environment. In order to temporarily restore coordination, inquiry searches for the best action to take at that moment. For Dewey, "All deliberation is a search for a *way* to act, not for a final terminus."[11] Inquiry is not merely at the level of the individual mind but the action occurring between organism and environment.

The process of inquiry entails deliberation. Deliberation is an experimental practice of investigating which combinations of habits, impulses, and objective environs produce viable actions for addressing and alleviating the problem. These are experiments of reasoning. Dewey claims,

We do not act *from* reasoning; but reasoning puts before us objects which are not directly or sensibly present, so that we then may react directly to these objects, with aversion, attraction, indifference or attachment, precisely as we would to the same objects if they were physically present.[12]

Reason, then, enables us to envision possible objects or states of affairs and to imagine what the best course of action might be given these objects. Hence, it enables us to reconstruct our habits in the present given the likelihood of situations in the future and the consequences of our past acts. Dewey reminds us that, while the foresight guiding this conceptual work is important, we cannot fully predict the future, nor should we try, for our inquiry should ultimately be concerned with the situation at the moment. Or, in Dewey's words, "foresight which draws liberally upon the lessons of past experience reveals the tendency, the meaning, of present action; and, once more, it is this present meaning rather than the future outcome which counts."[13]

Once we have envisioned reasonable courses of action, we extend the experiment to the actual situation by trying out these actions in small parts and observing their consequences. As we examine the act and its consequences, we gather facts about the situation that we can then interpret and reflect on. As we think further about the situation in light of these facts, our thought experiments, and the aspects of the situation that render it problematic, we create a hypothesis. This hypothesis takes shape not merely as an intellectual thought but as a mode of action that adjusts both ourselves and our environment, hence affecting the entire transactive encounter. When the hypothesis is deployed, we observe the consequences to determine whether coordination has been restored — whether a fruitful and just result has been achieved. If so, the inquiry has been successful, and we go about our lives. If not, we must consider and test alternative courses of action until we find one that works.

Because habit is "an acquired predisposition to *ways* or modes of response," hypothesis formation and testing as a search for ways to act almost always requires some consideration of and change in habit. Inquiry, itself a learned approach to problem solving, renders habits intelligent. This process brings into question some contemporary assumptions about habit as subconscious and distinct from or perhaps even immune to conscious reflection. Dewey claims that "'consciousness,' whether as a stream or as special sensations and images, expresses functions of habits, phenomena of their formation, operation, their interruption and reorganization."[14] Conscious thought, then, is never removed from habits, though the relation may be second order. When deliberation occurs, consciousness must necessarily consider some of one's habits in order to make sense of one's interactions with the problematic situation. Our habits are never entirely transparent to us, however. We assign certain meanings or privileges to some of our habits that might be perceived quite differently by other people. We can never achieve an objective perspective on our habits. And we can never reflect on all our habits all at once because thinking itself is a function of habits. Thinking requires some habits to be acting uninterrupted in order for thinking to continue. Additionally, some habits may be so engrained, others so taken for granted, and still others so deeply buried that bringing them into conscious reflection is very difficult.

Because bodily habits are the mediating platform between our thoughts and the world around us, Dewey's account of inquiry places them center stage. He claims that habits provide our thoughts a means of execution.[15] Habits are the everyday ways in which we carry out our intentions and the tools used to interact with and process our environment. Considering this in terms of consciousness, Sullivan intriguingly argues,

> Consciousness must now be thought of as an instrument of bodying, as an extension of bodily activity that is an aide to bodily reeducation, however, not as the taskmaster that will, apart from a body's habits, coerce a body into a new comportment. Likewise, agency must be rethought in terms of bodily effects, practices, and habits, rather than in terms of noncorporeal forces.[16]

Consciousness, then, is indivisible from the body and its habits. For Sullivan, as for me, the transactional relationship between the conscious and the subconscious in terms of habit explains how both bodily engagement with the world and the world itself can be changed.[17]

Such a suggestion goes against contemporary beliefs in the sole power of the intellect and systems of belief to assuage problems, including, for my purposes here, racism and sexism. Those theories are limited because they overlook the central role of bodily habit in the conceptual consideration of the world and the testing of solutions. They assign too much weight to the intellect without considering habit as a powerful force of mediation and initiative. Moreover, they do not see how habits can be, as Dewey calls them, artful— how they can be creative and make the most of a situation or the materials available.[18] Finally, when it comes to racism and sexism, they do not see how a willful change in beliefs regarding race and gender is ineffective unless accompanied by changes in the way one inhabits one's own race or gender or one's habitual responses to those of other people. When changing racist or sexist beliefs in this way, Dewey, though describing movements much different than social justice, rightly warns that

> a social revolution may effect abrupt and deep alterations in external customs, in legal and political institutions. But the habits that are behind these institutions and that have, willy-nilly, been shaped by objective conditions, the habits of thought and feeling, are not so easily modified. They persist and insensibly assimilate to themselves the outer innovations.[19]

Hence, legal and institutional measures designed to end racism and sexism often do not fully consider the staying power of some habits. Additionally, some
habits usurp well-intended initiatives, manipulating the new proposals until
they fill the needs of the stagnant habits. Habits related to white privilege, for
instance, have impacted and in some cases usurped affirmative action legislation or practice in hierarchies, privilege, and the centering of white demands
and experience. The success of these initiatives depends on reshaping the
habits behind institutions, including the ways in which people, especially
business and educational leaders, perceive and interact with candidates whose
backgrounds are different from their own.

Also important is the role of habit change in the meaning assigned to
events, beliefs, and bodies. Gert Biesta and Nicholas Burbules explain,

> What is special about the process of inquiry is that the (habitual) existential op-
> erations are in a sense "embedded" in a conceptual network. Because of this, the
> process of inquiry has a double outcome: There is not only a change in the habits
> of the organism, but also a change in the relationship between symbols, or in
> other words, a new *meaning*. After all, if it has been proven that we can act on
> *x* as meaning *y*, then this now means—on the conceptual level—that *x* now also
> has *y* as one of its possible meanings.[20]

When habits and their interaction with the social world are understood to bear
gender and racial meaning, the ability of inquiry to change these meanings
also becomes clear and significant. Such inquiry suggests new ways for transforming the ways in which we understand our raced and gendered selves as
well as those of others. Social customs of race or gender discrimination assume that repetition of racist or sexist habits will continue to repeat in the
same way. When the content or style of repetition is altered through inquiry,
these habits and their troubling meanings might be transformed.

As I noted at the beginning of this section, change of habit through inquiry
is only one aspect of flexible habits. Certainly intelligent inquiry is not required, and adopting a reading of Dewey that overemphasizes the intellectual
aspects of habit would offer far less rich an account of the staying power and
potential for change in race and gender than is offered by flexible habits. For
flexible habits also prize the processes of transformation that can though do
not necessarily require intelligent reflection, namely, parody, subversion, and
playfulness. To the extent that these subversive acts often pop up suddenly
through the play of language or when certain conditions arise, they still entail
predispositions to ways of being and are therefore often habitual yet do not
involve the detailed process of inquiry. These acts can beneficially direct and
redirect one's overarching habits, one's interactions with others, or the language that describes these activities. Without leading or demanding any type

of formal inquiry, teachers can at least emphasize these moments when they happen on their own.

REWORKING HABIT

While inquiry and playful parody can produce change of habits, habits can also be reworked in other ways. According to Dewey, change of habits cannot be targeted directly. Dewey claims, "We cannot change habit directly: that notion is magic. But we can change it indirectly by modifying conditions, by an intelligent selecting and weighting of the objects which engage attention and which influence the fulfillment of desires."[21] We must often investigate the conditions that cause certain habits to be formed or enacted. Of course, we usually must do so from within those very conditions. We can then modify the conditions that effect and enable our habits by intelligently reconstructing material objects and social relations. Like inquiry, this is also an experimental practice that requires careful observation of actions and consequences.

Often when rigid habits conflict or when a new environment is encountered, an impulse is released that deviates from custom and demands a change in habit. Dewey emphasizes impulses as key factors in the reworking of habit. He says, "Impulses are the pivots upon which the re-organization of activities turn, they are agencies of deviation, for giving new directions to old habits and changing their quality."[22] As I described in chapter 2, Dewey believes that impulses can be innovative sources for changing one's self and one's environment. But even while impulses may pose new directions for our habits, Dewey rightly claims that old habits are replaced by new variations; they are not shaken off entirely. As I argued in chapter 2, habits are constitutive for Dewey—they constitute us as recognizable beings who frame and pursue purposes. Habits are necessary. When a habit becomes problematic, it should be replaced.

Habits are often held as constellations—as groupings of habits the provide one with a sense of self. Each habit may take on varying significance in terms of race, gender, class, sexuality, and other identity markers when enacted in different situations or relative to other habits within its group. While habits are often held as a cluster, they typically change one aspect at a time through the process of inquiry or the provocation of impulse. Importantly, however, many people fear changing one of their habits because they suspect the whole system will come crashing down. These fears are indicative of the complex ways in which habits signify and interact with others clustered habits. In the case of gender and race, people may worry that changing one aspect of their gender or race, perhaps the way they talk or walk, jeopardizes their larger sense of self or identity. While a legitimate concern, this does not necessarily have to be the case.

Let's consider an example. Andre is an African American teenager who loves music. On a Saturday, you are likely to find him scratching records with black friends or playing around with the drums at the local music store. At school, he often slows his pace as he passes by the orchestra room and strains his ears to listen to the music inside. The principal at his school recently met with the orchestra conductor to discuss the lack of racial diversity in the organization. He suggested that the members may be telling nonwhites that they are not welcome to join. The conductor, offended, retorted that no minority students had asked to join in the first place.

Vivian Gussin Paley and other educational researchers have investigated the racial dynamics of group formation similar to those under question in this instance. In her work *You Can't Say You Can't Play*, for example, Paley studies the ways children choose to invite some peers to join their playgroups and dissuade others from doing so. Paley and others have not considered how habits may factor into these scenarios. Andre might enjoy playing the violin and may have even considered taking it up before. But as a racial minority in this genre and because of the musical expectations of his peers, Andre may lack the habits and environmental conditions necessary for violin playing to be a viable or desirable choice. Moreover, he may worry that playing violin will jeopardize his blackness insofar as it is enacted through a coherent, recognizable set of habits that perhaps do not include the playing of classical stringed instruments. If, however, change is understood in terms of small aspects of one's habits rather than entire identity sets, change may be viewed as more viable and appealing. Andre's current musical habits (including his proclivities for certain genres and his dexterity in manipulating their respective instruments) and the sense of self that relates to them might be modified to include the violin. Playing violin, then, would not require Andre to forsake his blackness but rather would change or expand one of the cultural habits of blackness.

SEDIMENTATION

The example of Andre raises concerns with the apparent limits of reworking habit due to the constraints of cultural norms and the possibility of habit sedimentation. These norms may foreclose certain ways of being and may lead others to appear as though natural and fixed—as I described in Butler's work in the previous chapter. I believe that Dewey rightly locates the source of these cultural norms:

We often fancy that institutions, social custom, collective habit, have been formed by the consolidation of individual habits. In the main this supposition is false to fact. To a considerable extent customs, or widespread uniformities of habit, exist because individuals face the same situation and react in like fashion. But to a larger extent customs persist because individuals form their personal habits under conditions set by prior customs.[23]

Shared cultural structures, then, come about not because people display similar habits but because they encounter similar objective conditions and prior customs. Andre and his friends, for example, are likely to have grown up hearing similar music played in their homes and seeing exclusively white orchestras (if they saw orchestras at all). This perspective on culture compliments both the Deweyan and the Butlerian theory of subjectivation, where subjects are constituted by their environments rather than ready-made originators of culture.

Bourdieu and the Constraints of the Habitus

Bourdieu also lends insight into the ways in which culture can thoroughly impact habits and lead to their sedimentation via the habitus. The socially acquired habitus manifests itself in embodied actions, behaviors, and tendencies. However, it is not reducible to these manifestations. The habitus takes bodily shape and has corporeal impact in many of the same ways that my notion of habit does. It is this bodily aspect that is particularly noteworthy. Butler praises Bourdieu's habitus because it shows how we unintentionally incorporate social norms into our everyday being.[24] It shows how cultural norms shape our bodies and guide their conduct in ways that are socially acceptable. Additionally, like Dewey's account of habit, Bourdieu's notion of habitus introduces a temporal, corporeal element of bodily living that is often lacking in the work of Foucault on gender identity and sometimes in the more linguistic-centered work of Butler. The deeply engrained bodily aspect of habitus and its hesitancy to change show why change is difficult and why more voluntarist notions of change like Foucault's practices of the self are limited or faulty ways of envisioning identity change.

For Bourdieu, identity can become sedimented by the ongoing force of the fields in which it is located and by the entrenchment of ways of being. The habitus is consolidated and reinforced through our experiences over time. It becomes fixed as children strive to achieve social, cultural, symbolic, or economic capital and discover that certain ways of being allow them to secure these ends. I would add here that those people of particular interest to my project on flexibility might be those minority races and genders who do not achieve these forms of capital in any thoroughgoing or enduring way. Because of this, their habitus may not become fixed in the same problematic ways that those of many capital-achieving, majority people are. It may be, then, that whites and other dominant groups have inflexible habits, while minorities have learned to be quite flexible in order to survive with or without capital.

Butler and many other critics claim that Bourdieu focuses too much on how the habitus is formed and becomes fixed than on how it can be changed. Hence, he provides a way of understanding the embodied living of race and gender norms but not a way of changing them or having agency within their confines. Agreeing with these critiques, I also claim that the body, for Bourdieu, comes to bear history but not challenge it. The body can only inadvertently expose the problems of social life, including racism and sexism, when it slips up, makes mistakes, or fails to behave appropriately. And because Bourdieu strongly maintains that the habitus and its effects remain at the subconscious level, there is only a slim chance that these failures will bring the social problems they may indicate to light. I use transaction as the key aspect of flexible habits to show that the process of forming the subject is also one of constant change. Moreover, I contend that habits can be targeted and consciously scrutinized to expedite change rather than simply to reveal problems by chance.

While habitus is overwhelmingly guided and constrained by early experiences, Bourdieu does allow that it can be affected by current environmental interaction. He says that habitus "is an open system of dispositions that is constantly subjected to experiences, and therefore constantly affected by them in a way that either reinforces or modifies its structures."[25] In this regard, habitus is affected. However, he also claims that the habitus is not always determinative but can be generative because it can actively impact the environment. He argues that because habitus is part of a field, it can exert force within that field, thereby affecting the environment. While such claims bear similarity to my description of transaction, Bourdieu gives little insight into how habitus can be generative and open. Indeed, across his works, his description of it appears largely conservative—as though the habitus is imported from cultural norms and must routinely reenact and reestablish those norms.

While he rightly notes that political protest must be collective, Bourdieu does not provide a basis for contestation or resistance within the habitus of the individual that would serve as a springboard for such action. He also does not show how identity sedimentation or problematic social structures can be revealed and reworked. It would seem that this would occur when people move between different fields, as it does happen when one's habits suddenly stand out or are called into question when one moves to a new environment. My notion of flexible habits also gets at this more tentative, shifting sense of identity that changes with new environments and uses these changes to overcome past and prevent future sedimentation. I offer a sense of change that is not a radical break with the past but rather a spiraling variation of habitual ways of being that changes other habits and the environment with each revolution. It is a change that arises out of and is not entirely distinct from the past. Finally, through the cultivation of flexible habits and certain habits of protest within individual students, I suggest that collective social and political change can begin. Bourdieu, on the other hand, would likely not see schools as capable of guiding the habitus toward breaking down inequalities or directing other social change. Schools, in his eyes, would merely provide a field for developing and maintaining a socially accepted habitus within each student. Schools would limit and further entrench the habitus. Bourdieu helpfully shows that schools are a large part of the problem as they currently stand. While this fact somewhat tempers my optimism regarding their ability to be a key part of the solution, it inspires me to rethink schools in new ways that are instrumental in social transformation.

Rupturing Sedimentation

Even though habits appear to be constrained by the cultural norms that may have partially produced them, Dewey's transactional philosophy leaves open the possibility for change. When habits are invoked in contexts different from the ones in which they were created, their transactional relationship with their new environment may, at minimum, suggest a problem within that space or may lead to revision of the original habits. Even without a change in environment, habit is likely not to be entirely sedimented. Habits often appear identically repetitive, but each time they seem to copy their prior activity or that of others, they often do not mimic the original exactly. This variation on repetition allows for the habits themselves to undermine sedimentation and to bring about slow change.

As I described briefly in the previous chapter, Butler posits a bodily excess that can rupture sedimentation. This excess exceeds interpellation and can trouble performances by varying the context, content, or style of their repetition in unexpected ways. Inspired by Dewey, Sullivan argues that this explanation is "more misleading than helpful; it suggests a static, separate thing that stands apart from social performatives and habits and attempts to disrupt them from without, rather than suggesting the transactional process of actively remaking itself."[26] In this regard, I think Sullivan is correct. Positing an excess that is itself outside the realm of the habitual is nonsensical and unhelpful.

Like Sullivan, I find it useful to consider Deweyan impulse as capable of disrupting sedimentation. Impulses can be conceived of as sparks that strike out in new directions or provoke change in habits. In the end, however, Sullivan concludes that the concept of impulse cannot support Butler's depiction of bodily excess because impulse cannot meaningfully be separated from habit under Dewey's scheme.

Sullivan believes that impulse is ineffective unless organized by habit.[27] I disagree. I want to suggest instead that impulse as unaffiliated may be precisely that which provokes habit reformation in some cases. Impulse can be related to and yet not be fully pinned down as habit, thereby serving as a fire poker to urge habits to organize or be carried out in new ways. Just because habit and impulse cannot be meaningfully separated does not mean that impulse cannot act as legitimate or useful excess in certain moments that upset sedimentation. Dewey describes this capacity as he argues that evolution does not mean humans are progressing toward a given or natural end—a final, fixed way of being: "Significant stages in change are found not in access of fixity of attainment but in those crises in which a seeming fixity of habits gives way to a release of capacities that have not previously functioned."[28] Impulses are these capacities, these bodily excesses, that confound their contextual environment. And while they often take us off guard because they surpass our current self-understanding, they may be harnessed into habits in ways that still allow us to be active in our self-reformation as Sullivan rightly desires. Or, in Dewey's words, "Impulse is a source, an indispensable source, of liberation; but only as it is employed in giving habits pertinence and freshness does it liberate power."[29]

For Dewey, there is always a waiting pool of impulses that have not yet come into play:

> There always exists a goodly store of non-functioning impulses which may be drawn upon. Their manifestation and utilization is called conversion or generation when it comes suddenly. But they may be drawn upon continuously and moderately. Then we call it learning or educative growth. Rigid custom signifies not that there are no such impulses but that they are not organically taken advantage of. As a matter of fact, the stiffer and the more encrusted the customs, the larger is the number of instinctive activities that find no regular outlet and that accordingly merely await a chance to get an irregular, uncoordinated manifestation.[30]

Impulses, then, can come into play suddenly on their own or be carefully drawn out and capitalized on through the process of education. Rigid customs, like those that form and maintain the habitus, avoid and suppress impulses that are seen as threatening. However, flexible habits work to use them as agents of change. Just as cultural norms appear static and ways of being appear permanently sedimented, so do bodily habits, yet when the flexibility of habits is revealed and invoked, each is opened to reworking and resignification.

DEFINING FLEXIBLE HABITS

While Dewey appreciates the plasticity of humans and the habits that constitute them, he does not describe them using the term I have developed: "flexible habits." He illustrates how habits change through processes of conflict and inquiry but does not fully theorize how habit itself can be inherently flexible—how the process of transaction, the irritating force of impulse, and the need for successful traversal of the world relate to flexible habits. Nonetheless, my sense of flexible habits grows out of Dewey's philosophy and is informed by Butler's theories on power, subjectivity, performativity, and political insurrection.

Flexible habits can be understood in two ways. In one regard, they are habits characterized by flexibility: ease of adapting to unexpected situations, openness to new ideas, and the like. In another sense, paradoxical as it may seem given the common use of "habit," the habits *themselves* are flexible. It is in this sense that Dewey's unique understanding of habit is especially useful. In this case, good or flexible habits allow themselves to be altered when they prove to be no longer satisfactory in a situation. They are tentative, though not to the extent of jeopardizing the entire self they constitute, for they cannot be changed all at once. Certain habits (which may themselves later be changed) serve as launching points for the reworking of old and developing of new habits.

Flexible habits are sensitive to the nuances of material, social, and linguistic contexts and allow one to operate with ease as environments shift. Flexible habits are those that predispose one to change—to striking out in new directions and to trying out new modes of living. Darwinian in some regards, flexible habits are those the adoption and adaptation of which secure the well-being of the species, though these habits are assessed by ecologically minded pragmatic principles of just flourishing for all. Even as change is a key aspect of flexible habits, they retain the repetitive nature of habits. They are often intimately corporeal and unconscious, though they exhibit a greater ease for being called into consciousness and scrutinized than their more rigid counterparts.

While not a wholesale change of the self, employing flexible habits can promote particular, context-specific change and foster growth. Here, growth should be understood in a Deweyan sense, as growth that is not necessarily linear and lacks teleology. Growth describes how continuous experiences can develop our physical, intellectual, and moral capacities—actualizing them and helping them inform one another so that they continue in a chain that enables one to live satisfactorily. This sense of growth is lacking in Butler's account of performativity. Dewey goes on to explain that "all habit has *continuity*, and while a flexible habit does not secure in its operation bare recurrence nor absolute assurance neither does it plunge us into the hopeless confusion of the absolutely different."[31] Flexible habits bring about change without jeopardizing growth and continuity. Growth expresses the movement invoked by experience, which compounds on itself. And freedom depends on the continued development and growth of experience.[32] Insofar as Dewey conceives of freedom as the ability to change oneself, to frame purposes in the world, and to enact environmental change, flexible habits are central to achieving this goal.

Habits of flexibility include openness to others, imagination, holding one's beliefs tentatively, ease of meeting new people, conscious reflection on oneself, bodily comportment that welcomes communication, comfortably adapting to unexpected situations, and accommodating difference. These are habits to the extent that they predispose us to act and to be sensitive to certain internal and environmental phenomena without dictating exactly what the content of our response must be. As flexible habits, however, even those listed here must be held tentatively—capable of being reformed and replaced when they prove to be problematic. They must be held in ways that provide structure and a sense of self while also being dynamic. While this may appear to be a contradiction, emphasis on a Deweyan account of transaction and a Butlerian sense of fluidity recasts the relationship between a sufficiently stable self and the world around it, highlighting this as a desirable possibility rather than an incongruity.

Although habits of flexibility may appear as perennially good, perhaps even virtuous in some regards, there may be a few instances where the more appropriate or ethical response to a race or gender problem is to replace these habits with ones that are more resolute. This could occur when a white person is being persuaded or even recruited by a racial extremist. Rather than being open-minded and inviting of discussion, it may be more appropriate to resolutely turn one's back and walk away. Likewise, when black students encounter institutionalized racism in schools, resolute resistance may be needed. While to some extent a strategy for dealing with racism, these actions are habits in that they are patterns of impulses that are working capacities, provoking fruitful action and change in the environment.

My notion of agency via flexible habit both challenges and extends Dewey's philosophy in terms of identity and agency. Dewey does not fully theorize how habits enact our races and genders and how hierarchies of race and gender are built on our habitual responses to race and gender. Because he does not consider how these habits congeal into culturally recognizable ways of being that can problematically become inhibiting, he does not consider the implications of flexible habits for reworking identity.

Dewey, despite upholding habits as changeable, at times poses a problematic core of habits that abides.[33] This core provides one the identity and sense of self that he believes is necessary for enacting positive freedom (as the ability to frame purposes relative to one's capacities) and is a critical facet of deliberation. For Dewey, identities teach us about ourselves and options available to us. Framing and enacting aims requires a strong, coherent sense of self. Indeed, he calls for learning situations that focus on our identities and urge us to express ourselves.[34] While Dewey allows that even this core is a contingent cultural product that may be changed over time, he seems to cherish it in ways that I believe overlook how that core may be complicit in oppressive acts toward others or in stagnant notions of one's self or one's identity group.

Butler provocatively asks, "To what extent is 'identity' a normative ideal rather than a descriptive feature of experience?"[35] As described earlier, Butler reveals the constraining and essentializing ways in which subjects are pressured to fulfill identities. For Butler, this activity is—and should be—doomed to fail. In order to enhance agency, Butler insists that we need to forgo our efforts to maintain stable categories of self-identity. We must be willing to be interpellated within and outside the categories in which we envision ourselves so that we may subversively misrecognize and misrepresent them. Hence, Butler presents identity construction as a political process and identity as a political effect, thereby offering up new matter for political change and complicating Dewey's goal of individual identity development and maintenance. She locates a fruitful future in relinquishing coherence. This suggestion is well aligned with the notion of agency as power redeployment, which does not require internal coherence to be achieved. Following Butler in this regard, I would urge Dewey to go one step farther in his support of elastic habits—to trace them all the way down to reveal that fundamental defining identities are not necessary. I would also push the Deweyan conception of transaction to be more thoroughgoing by upholding stability only as relative to specific moments and situations rather than as an abiding goal or need.

ACHIEVING BUTLER'S GOALS

Even while taking slightly different shapes than Butler's project, flexible habits are still able to achieve many of Butler's goals I described in chapter 4.

I described some of the relations between flexible habits and these goals previously but add a few more remarks to better explain how my project supplements and extends that of Butler.

Habits, like gender for Butler, are a doing. Focusing attention on the habits of gender can reveal gender as a socially molded activity, but flexible habits can also offer more. Insofar as flexible habits arise from and are continually checked by intelligent inquiry, they can enable us to do gender differently and to expose the faulty edges of current gender definitions. They offer a platform for this insurrectionary work that is intimately organic, embodied, and connected to the environment while simultaneously shaped by pragmatic notions of good living. While flexible habits may continue to engage in repetition, the habits themselves and their effects can always be changed. This shifting, tentative nature helps prevent the problematic gender sedimentation Butler identifies from occurring.

Butler says that attributes that do not conform to the standards of intelligibility for men and women as substances can debunk the coherence and acceptability of such notions of substance.[36] Flexible habits are capable of achieving this. In Gail Boldt's classroom described earlier, students discussed gendered standards by listing the traits of idealized gender groups. However, they ignored moments when they themselves or some of their peers violated or contradicted those norms through their behavior, appearance, or activity.[37] Teachers can focus student attention on the unique habits of individuals, perhaps by using members of the school whose habits sometimes wander outside the bounds of femininity or masculinity as praiseworthy rather than exhibitionary examples. A teacher might highlight, for example, a boy in the class who enjoys playing a traditionally female sport or a girl who likes wearing the jerseys of her favorite football team. Through such examples, it may become more clear to students that gender is not coherent and that idealized definitions of gender do not match the lives of real people whose interests and activities tend to have both traditionally male and female aspects. Moreover, children may come to see that the lives of those with flexible habits are particularly difficult to encapsulate by gender categories.

When insistence on the coherence of one's subject position is relinquished, one is better able to see the complexity within oneself and how that complexity entails the lives of others.[38] Thereby, one may be led to living more justly when those others are accounted for. Moreover, when such investigation is conducted in the classroom, students can also explore the ways in which gender should not be coherent insofar as coherence leads to normalization and exclusion. The proliferation of flexible habits can aid in fulfilling Butler's goal of maximizing the possibilities for livable life.[39] Interestingly, these possibilities may have existed all along and simply not been recognized.

It is likely the case that the law and cultural definitions of gender have upheld gendered images that adhere only to rigid habits or idealized traits. Propagating the investigation and cultivation of flexible habits in the classroom, however, will more centrally attune students to these alternatives and their value.

By making identities more flexible, they become less coherent and therefore are less likely to perpetuate radical exclusion. In an educational setting, the exclusions that they do continue can be scrutinized as to their problematic effects and reworked when needed for the sake of ethical democracy. Butler emphasizes the goal of citations revealing exclusion.[40] A pedagogy based on flexible habits can draw attention to the bodily activities or habits that cite officially proper movements or positions in ways that reveal what they have excluded. For example, students could be sensitized to moments like that described earlier where Annette takes on the authoritative role of team selector and assigns boys to different sporting teams. Annette is not simply repeating the role of captain, as many boys before her have done, but she does so while simultaneously juxtaposing her femaleness or, perhaps in her unique case, her nonmaleness. In this way, Annette carries out *"an insubordination that appears to take place within the very terms of the original*, effectively reintroducing or revealing that which has traditionally been excluded from the captain's position, the female, or at minimum, the non-biologically sexed male."[41] In some cases, exclusions can be addressed through classroom discussions and exercises. In this way, a pedagogy focused on bodily activity promotes a proliferation of genders and races in the present. It also reveals weaknesses in current gender and racial norms that can eventually entirely undermine these identities as well as identity-defined positions of privilege in the long run.[42]

Admittedly, I use the language of dispositions that Butler warns against. She argues that a focus on dispositions covers up their sources of prohibitions and prevents exploration into them.[43] But I conceive of habits as dispositions in ways that involve an intelligent working out of historicity in the classroom such that those sources are not only revealed but also discussed and troubled. The dialogic aspect of a pedagogy of flexible habits is important in this regard and others.

Many of the linguistic insurrections that Butler praises lead to linguistic disjoint, a moment where problems are revealed but not resolved. While these moments can certainly be of value for resignification and for troubling the definitions of identity categories and social norms, they often result in a paralyzing moment of impasse. Participants are unsure how to proceed once this moment occurs, and in many cases the dialogue that was in progress stops prematurely. For example, one high school teacher was discussing race with her students. She asked, "Do you all consider yourselves African-American?" "No," one boy replied sarcastically, "I'm a gorilla."[44] While this unexpected utterance valuably exposes one disturbing connotation of "African Ameri-can," it problematically stops the conversation. What might have been a pro-ductive conversation that worked through this statement was curtailed. A ped-agogy of flexible habits, however, fosters constructive communication, especially in the classroom, where teachers can identify these knotty mo-ments and guide students through them. Because flexible habits prize suc-cessful interaction, they must strive to continue communication until the problem has been resolved or coordinated action has been restored.

This coordinated action is the heart of communication for Dewey. Because communication is more than the exchange of information but action together, effective communication entails anticipating an interlocutor's actions and re-sponding to the meaning of his or her acts.[45] When dialogic partners are con-fronted with a difficult situation and inquiry is provoked, changing oneself of-ten relies on or is aided by the observations of others. When one's partner communicates these observations through the way that he or she physically and linguistically engages the situation, personal change becomes a more so-cial process. This is markedly different from what may be perceived to be a politics of the individual in Butler's work, yet it is a more educative and fruit-ful way for achieving many of the goals she names.

NOTES

1. Debra Van Ausdale and Joe R. Feagin, *The First R: How Children Learn Race and Racism* (Lanham, Md.: Rowman & Littlefield, 2001), 48–50.
2. John Dewey, "Racial Prejudice and Friction," in *The Middle Works of John Dewey*, vol. 13, ed. Jo Ann Boydston (1921; reprint, Carbondale: Southern Illinois University Press, 1988), 243.
3. This observation would sound a bit silly if it were not for my alma mater's bas-ketball team leading the country while they and their fans sport orange outfits.
4. Audre Lorde, *Sister Outsider* (Freedom, Calif.: Crossing Press, 1984), 147–48, quoted in Van Ausdale and Feagin, *The First R*, 88–89.
5. Dewey, "Racial Prejudice and Friction," 243.
6. Dewey, "Racial Prejudice and Friction," 244.
7. Dewey, "Racial Prejudice and Friction," 246.
8. It is unclear what would happen at the end of this period, whether racial groups would be able to re-self-segregate but remain no longer prejudiced against other groups or whether the privileging of one's own group would recede and people would choose to remain intermixed.
9. Sullivan does an excellent job of showing, via W. E. B. DuBois, that Dewey's assumption that all people are leery of those different from themselves may result from Dewey's projection of his position of white privilege onto others. It follows from her argument that aversion may be a white experience of the foreign and that

Dewey's depiction of the naturalness of antistrange feelings may serve to defend the ways in which whites have historically encountered and assimilated other races. Shannon Sullivan, "From the Foreign to the Familiar: Confronting Dewey Confronting Racial Prejudice," *Journal of Speculative Philosophy* 18, no. 3 (2004): 198.

10. John Dewey, *Logic: The Theory of Inquiry*, in *The Later Works of John Dewey*, vol. 12, ed. Jo Ann Boydston (1938; reprint, Carbondale: Southern Illinois University Press, 1994), 108 (italics in original), quoted in Gert J. J. Biesta and Nicholas C. Burbules, *Pragmatism and Educational Research* (Lanham, Md.: Rowman & Littlefield, 2003), 59.

11. John Dewey, *Human Nature and Conduct* (1922; reprint, Mineola, N.Y.: Dover, 2002), 193.

12. Dewey, *Human Nature and Conduct,* 200.

13. Dewey, *Human Nature and Conduct*, 208.

14. Dewey, *Human Nature and Conduct*, 177.

15. Dewey, *Human Nature and Conduct*, 30 and 67.

16. Shannon Sullivan, *Living across and through Skins: Transactional Bodies, Pragmatism, and Feminism* (Bloomington: Indiana University Press, 2001), 123.

17. Sullivan, *Living across and through Skins*, 77.

18. Dewey, *Human Nature and Conduct*, 77.

19. Dewey, *Human Nature and Conduct*, 108.

20. Biesta and Burbules, *Pragmatism and Educational Research*, 65.

21. Dewey, *Human Nature and Conduct*, 20.

22. Dewey, *Human Nature and Conduct*, 93.

23. Dewey, *Human Nature and Conduct*, 58.

24. Judith Butler, *Excitable Speech: A Politics of the Performative* (New York: Routledge, 1997), 142.

25. Pierre Bourdieu, *An Invitation to Reflexive Sociology* (Cambridge: Polity Press, 1992), 133.

26. Sullivan, *Living across and through Skins*, 103.

27. Sullivan, *Living across and through Skins*, 101.

28. Dewey, *Human Nature and Conduct*, 284.

29. Dewey, *Human Nature and Conduct*, 105.

30. Dewey, *Human Nature and Conduct*, 102–3.

31. Dewey, *Human Nature and Conduct*, 244.

32. John Dewey, *Experience and Education* (Indianapolis: Kappa Delta Pi, 1998), 28 and 40.

33. Dewey, *Experience and Education*, 38 and 43.

34. John Dewey, *Outlines of a Critical Theory of Ethics*, in *The Early Works of John Dewey*, vol. 3, ed. Jo Ann Boydston (1891; reprint, Carbondale: Southern Illinois University Press, 1969), 305.

35. Judith Butler, *Gender Trouble: Tenth Anniversary Edition* (New York: Routledge, 1999), 16.

36. Butler, *Gender Trouble*, 32.

37. Gail Masuchika Boldt, "Sexist and Heterosexist Responses to Gender Bending in an Elementary Classroom," *Curriculum Inquiry* 26, no. 2 (1996): 119.

38. Judith Butler, *Bodies That Matter: On the Discursive Limits of "Sex"* (New York: Routledge, 1993), 115.

39. We have to be careful here that this proliferation of alternatives does not bring about linguistic death. See Judith Butler, *Undoing Gender* (New York: Routledge, 2004), 8. This would happen when one's attributes so radically depart from standards of intelligibility that one is no longer discursively recognized. While flexible habits can display uniqueness and variation and can debunk coherence, they tend to be differences that arise gradually out of past forms rather than the drastic changes that might suddenly provoke annihilation.

40. Butler, *Bodies That Matter*, 45.

41. Butler, *Bodies That Matter* (italics in original).

42. Butler sets this goal in *Bodies That Matter*, 237.

43. Butler, *Gender Trouble*, 82.

44. Mica Pollock, *Colormute: Race Talk Dilemmas in an American School* (Princeton, N.J.: Princeton University Press, 2004), 31.

45. Biesta and Burbules, *Pragmatism and Educational Research*, 41.

Chapter Six

Cultivating Flexible Habits in Schools

While the past few chapters have explored the theoretical grounding of flexible habits, this chapter fleshes out a vision of what the cultivation of these habits might look like in the classroom. It explores some of the theoretical and practical ways in which teachers can cultivate flexible habits within the context of social justice education and classrooms concerned with issues of race and gender. To do so, I describe classroom situations and return to others recounted so far. I show both how these situations can be better understood through the theoretical lens I have offered and how these situations might be changed or improved through the cultivation of flexible habits. I also show how my account of flexible habits stems from some of these instances where flexible habits (particularly those of minority youth) are already operating.

CONTEMPORARY SCHOOLS

Bourdieu's account of the habitus provides helpful insight into the ways in which schools currently develop the habits of children. Schools produce dispositions and structures of understanding that enable children to navigate the world by becoming accustomed to the typical ways in which it operates. Over time, these dispositions crystallize into the habitus. The habitus bears a sense of social history and socializes children by internalizing cultural norms. This process of socialization results in the coordination of the beliefs and activities of the members of a society. Schools normalize children into certain standard ways of living (by learning common courtesies, social bureaucracy, and the like) and standard bases of knowledge (shared languages, handwriting systems, and other cultural knowledge codes). These normalizing processes are often good and justified practices. They orient children to the ways of the world and ensure that they learn how to operate within its confines. Schools strive to guarantee that children will have the knowledges and practices that will enable them to be productive workers, active citizens, and participants in cultural traditions. In many cases, these are valuable effects, and the habitus provides a theoretical concept for understanding how individuals come to embody these knowledges and dispositions.

Because of the importance of developing these shared habits, like methods and styles of communication that are firmly held by all students and graduates, it is necessary for me to recognize that schools cannot and should not develop flexible habits in every regard. There are some habits related to schooling that should be relatively stable throughout time and consistent across people. Indeed, schools are often rightfully in the business of developing rather rigid, normalized habits. Because schools have carried out this purpose for many years, institutional structures have been established that reinforce the development of some inflexible habits. Curricular and pedagogical practices have been developed that mimic, encompass, or reify the larger social field in order to ensure that basic skills and social knowledges will be thoroughly engrained. Standardized tests have been created to assess whether more academically based skills have been mastered. These structures pervade even some of the more mundane practices of schools, including the orderly ways in which children line up to move between classrooms, the organization of student desks in order to maintain the teacher's position of authority or the efficiency of classroom activity, the categorizing of student clubs and athletic teams in ways that mimic larger social groupings in the adult working world, and so on.

While these institutional structures for developing traditional social and intellectual habits are in many cases justified because they provide a foundation for communication and shared social experience, they pose many problems for the cultivation of flexible habits of gender and race. In some instances, these institutional forces may limit the development of flexible habits directly, though not always in openly explicit ways. As developers of habitus, these schools may so deeply entrench the social norms of the past that sedimentation becomes nearly inevitable and space for flexibility may be quite limited. In other instances, schools may be resistant to students' flexible habits insofar as they jeopardize the stability of the school itself. In still other instances, institutions may restrict flexible habits insofar as they perpetuate stagnant ways of being raced or gendered that run counter to the more flexible ways of being that individual teachers or classroom activities may seek to foster. They may not allow students' flexible habits to get off the ground because the setting reinforces more rigid boundaries of race and gender. These constraints may pose substantial limitations to a school's capacity to cultivate flexible habits at present.

Even as flexible habits may alleviate some political struggles and inequalities, they pose new challenges to schools and introduce some potential problems as schools must try to determine and reconcile which habits they should attempt to instill more rigidly and which more flexibly. As I argue in this chapter and have maintained in the previous chapters, to the extent that inhabiting race and gender in narrow and discrete ways brings about undeserved privileges for some groups, sets up barriers between people perceived as different, inhibits effective communication across difference, and maintains inequalities, these habits of identity should be more flexible. While inflexibly inhabiting race or gender may provide one with a stronger sense of a traditional self and may build some beneficial ground of solidarity with others, theses benefits are often overwhelmed by the social detriments just listed. With these limitations and practical problems in mind, the remainder of this chapter focuses on envisioning how a school whose institutional structures and goals were more supportive of flexible habits might function.

THE CONTEXT OF EDUCATION FOR FLEXIBLE HABITS

Before delving into the cultivation of flexible habits in the classroom, I must first address the larger context of such an educational endeavor. Dewey and Butler's ideas about democracy and social change as well as their theories of embodiment, in particular, are helpful for envisioning a broad picture of good education, especially an education attuned to issues of race and gender. Taken together, Butler and Dewey's theories of embodied living offer many prescriptive directions for educating embodied beings and begin to paint a picture of a classroom where flexible habits can be cultivated and supported.

Overall and from the start, the scope of education must be widened. As embodied and transactional, the ontological and ethical field of ourselves and our environment is made more level. This shifts the priorities in education and makes it more ecologically and environmentally conscious. Paradoxically, embodied education does not mean people-first education. Emphasizing transaction and ecology entails debunking the privilege of humanness and autonomy previously supported in education.[1] In addition to opening up schooling to include the larger environment, schools should also concern the larger student. Or, as Dewey says, "What we want is to have the child come to school with a whole mind and a whole body, and leave school with a fuller mind and an even healthier body."[2] Education is about improving the well-being of the mind, body, and surroundings, not only the intellect. Moreover, education is about situating the student in his or her entirety within an ecologically sound and ethically balanced environment.

Following from this expanded notion of education, the issues of education should be those encountered daily by individuals in a common setting and should involve the entire student. School subject material should be taken up into the child's experience via bodily activity, always arising out of and relating back to everyday embodied living. This is not only because children enjoy learning in this way but also, more fundamentally, because this is the way that children learn from their earliest days. Academic subjects should not be narrowly geared toward the mind, for the body and its preservation are a great source of motivation for learning, as is embodied joint activity with others. Course work that makes us sensitive to and aware of our bodies, including the ways in which they are constituted by social standards, should hold a special place in schools. This may include analysis of media representations of beautiful bodies or course work in drama or dance that attunes students to their bodily presentation.[3] As I argue later in this chapter, this aspect of education is especially pertinent to the development of flexible habits.

On an embodied view, schools, appropriately tasked with instilling and cultivating knowledge within students, should recognize that knowledge is not gathering facts apart from human experience. Knowledge is not accumulating facts that exist independently of human living. Rather, knowledge entails intelligently comprehending the embodied relation between agent and act, between bodies (including nonhuman ones) as activities and their consequences. Knowledge entails grasping and making meaning of the relations between experience and nature.[4]

Furthermore, the senses should not be devalued as simple transporters of knowledge or factual information to the mind. Instead, schools should more appropriately regard them as useful tools that give activity and meaning making purpose. Senses relate intellectual activity to engagement with the world in ways that emphasize the physical drive for sustenance and well-being. These motivations also render the senses sources for provoking activity, "as stimuli to action."[5]

Butler's process of deconstruction, in particular, could set a new agenda for embodied education. "To deconstruct is to acknowledge and to analyze the operations of exclusion, erasure, foreclosure and abjection in the discursive construction of the subject."[6] While politically risky, schools could engage students in these educative tasks by making them more aware of how and what their bodies signify and how they are implicated or complicit in the negative characterizations of some races and genders. When students become more aware of their embodied relatedness with others, they may become more aware of their social position, their role in maintaining hierarchies, and their ability to change the ways in which they live. The ability to make such change comes most centrally from and through the body, not just through political know-how or accumulation of knowledge. While recognizing cultural constructs and their constraints inherent within the school's institutional setting, classrooms might engage Dewey's question, "How might we fruitfully restructure the cultural constructs that shape the habits that we are?"[7] They might even push one step farther by actually carrying out such restructuring in order to alter students' habits.

HISTORY, LANGUAGE, AND IMAGES

Set within this broadened vision of education, a focus on bodily habit logically follows. For those who do not or cannot envision education as such, concerns with bodily habit still should not come as a surprise. Even within traditional teaching and socialization, habits have been key points in education. For years, teachers, especially in the elementary grades, have spent many hours addressing habits by molding the behaviors, dispositions, and comportment of children. Gail Boldt, for instance, describes a teacher who gets her young students to quiet down by drawing attention to the physical comportment of a boy who is quiet and listening well. She points out the way he sits, where he puts his hands, and how he acts toward others.[8] By praising his activities, the teacher effectively encourages the other students to develop habits of attentiveness and a polite, respectful demeanor. Most teachers are already aware of the body and how its habitual activity effects classroom learning. My project encourages teachers to think about those habits as raced and gendered and as appropriate targets of classroom teaching and learning. It depicts changes in identity and political forms through an elaborated approach of which many teachers, sometimes unknowingly, have been addressing the fundamentals for many years. My project is not a radical proposal. Rather, it is a rethinking of identity formation and inequality and an emphasis on the habits that sustain them within an approach—the cultivation of flexible habits—that, at its base, is already familiar to most teachers.

Existentialist philosopher of education Maxine Greene urges teachers to use aesthetic experiences to disturb students' traditional or debilitating habits. Building from Greene, I explore the ways in which history, literature, language, art, and performance can be used to creatively spark introspection and promote the development of flexible habits.

First, classroom work on habits of race and gender may be introduced through engagement with history. In an approach similar to my reflections on the history of science in chapter 3, classes might explore the historical ways in which habits have defined race and gender. While it may seem that such a subject must be artificially introduced, attuning students to their own struggles with racial and gender identification will likely reveal that students are already confronting identity issues that either already entail a historical component or can be better addressed through historical analysis. In the classroom of high school teacher Mica Pollock, for example, a fight broke out between black and Latino students.[9] Many of the slurs and verbal insults exchanged expressed both student knowledge and confusion regarding the naturalness of group distinction. Rather than curtailing the argument and effectively ignoring it by continuing with academic work, Pollock engaged this event historically. She led the class in discussing the label "Latino." By highlighting common assumptions about the natural distinctions of groups and tracing their histories, Pollock revealed that "Latino" is a social construction. Within such an investigation, Pollock and teachers like her could examine the effects of this social construction over time on the constitution and performance of the body while simultaneously highlighting how the concept of race has declined in scientific validity. Teachers might also emphasize the ways in which schools currently perpetuate "Latino" categories and points of difference by requiring parents to indicate the race of their children on enrollment forms and by encouraging Latino children to join the Latino/Latina Club. Classes might also discuss the effects of educational policies like No Child Left Behind that require students to be discretely separated into racial groups in order to assess their performance relative to others. Such a discussion may help students and teachers better understand constraints within their own institution that hinder the achievement of flexible identities.[10]

I would encourage teachers to explore the history of the words and identity categories assigned to races and genders. Some words, like "dominant" or "majority," invoke power as well as a history of control and are often tied to descriptions of white people.[11] Other words produce harm. Teachers could point to injurious words and explain their histories, possibly revealing their potential for harm as well as ways that they might be misappropriated to break the link between the word and its harm. The history of the word "nigger," including its offensive past and recent reclamation within some circles, could serve as an excellent example for such a classroom activity. Of course, engaging this word must be done delicately, and teachers must be prepared for some reservations on the part of students, parents, and administrators. Introduction to this topic certainly need not be arbitrary, however; it could stem from insults uttered in the school yard or from analysis of lingo and music heard openly in school halls. A teacher might draw on sources as diverse as *Huckleberry Finn,* documents of the civil rights era, or contemporary rap music to investigate this tumultuous history with the class. As we have seen in the example of the boy who describes other students as variations of "pinos" and the incident of the African American student who proclaimed himself to be a gorilla, some students are already aware of the importance of identity terms, their capacity to harm, and their ability to be reworked. Overt discussions of these incidents and the terms they draw into question may beneficially reveal the histories of identity terms, including their changes over time and their instability for the future. Racial references to gorillas, then, might evoke a now debunked history of scientific classification that is a shared knowledge in the classroom. The parody of a student who labels himself in this way could then be taken up in beneficial ways in such a historically attuned classroom.

Racial and gender slurs are relatively common in schools throughout the United States. Whether the whispered insult of "stupid nigger" by a white child toward a singing black girl or the forceful belittling shout of "Paki!" from a white boy attacking a South Asian boy on the playground, verbal insults occur regularly in many classrooms. Often, as was the case with both of these playground instances, these insults either go unheard by teachers or are ignored. When they are acknowledged, most teachers hush the student issuing them, deliver a reprimand, or curtail the speaker in another way. Few teachers engage these occurrences in ways that might more productively alter the situations.

I contend that teachers should help students see that when they cite a racial or gender slur, they become inducted into a certain historical linguistic community, whether that be one of racists or sexists.[12] The term they use deploys a history of harm and force that is garnered by this community. Butler notes, "When the injurious term injures (and let me make clear that I think it does), it works its injury precisely through the accumulation and dissimulation of its force. The speaker who utters the racial slur is thus citing that slur, making linguistic community with a history of speakers."[13] Butler also explains how hate speech never stems only from one person but from a community that gives the citation of a racial or gender slur its efficacy. Given this, racism or sexism should be thought of not as systems maintained by discrete individuals but rather as communities that are perpetuated through discursive and performative citations of their past harm. Working against racism and sexism, then, should be a project not of simply changing individuals but of dismantling these larger communities by undermining the citations that propagate them. When students become habitually prone to citing racial or gender slurs, their affinity with this community grows stronger. And when students become plagued by a tendency to employ such language, a bad habit—one that blocks ethical communication and transaction with people different from themselves—may take

hold. Teachers can expose the pitfalls of this community, making students uncomfortable with their linguistic connection to it.

Additionally, the teacher and other members of the classroom can contest the
particular slur in ways that help prevent the repetition of such slurs from achieving the injury they espouse.[14] As we saw earlier in the case of the young biracial Pakistani boy, Stephen is able to disrupt the racially demeaning language
revolving around being called a "Pakistan." He introduces recent history, the
success of the Pakistani cricket team, to deflate the potency of the insult and actually uplift his identity group as one of pride and worthy of desire. Simultaneously, Stephen troubles Jordan's affiliation with the racist community of sports
players evident on the racially divided playground of the British school by
showing that members of his nation have succeeded at a task valued by that
community. Future slurs regarding sporting weakness aimed at Prajay and other
Pakistani boys in the future may, then, not bear as much injury as they once did.

As classes explore the historical aspects of racial and gender slurs, identity
terms, and other forms of linguistic description, they might also consider the
images that relate to or that are evoked by these words. A class may, for example, study the image of the savage that was attributed to Irish and blacks
many years ago in order to better understand how this image shored up the
privileged vision of whiteness. Class members could study artists' depictions
of these "savage" populations and those of white nobility in western Europe
as well as journals of explorers and traders.

Images could also be studied as changing over time or varying by context.
Robin Good, for example, discusses four images of black women and their
problematic histories. She shows how the images of Mammy, Patriarch, Wel-
fare Mother, and Jezebel (sexually aggressive woman or whore) have arisen
during certain historical periods influenced by the contextual factors of slavery, economics, and sexual morality. Contemporary racial descriptions of
crack mothers, jokes about spending checks on the first of the month, or Aunt
Jemima insults often allude to or support these images. Good proposes an intriguing educational exercise to explore and combat these images. She suggests playing blues that is written and performed by black women in the
classroom. She suggests that classes should discuss this music, which she believes reveals the oppression of black women as well as how those women
envision themselves—images quite different from those controlling ones that
"replicate privilege and oppression."[15] Encountering these alternative images
may goad students into reconsidering the stereotypical images they hold and
how these images may problematically impact their interactions with people
different from themselves. Advanced classes might further investigate whose
interests are served by the dominant images as well as how and why they have
been perpetuated throughout history.

Troubling racial and gender descriptions and images through historical analysis can be a fruitful endeavor for targeting the contemporary ways in which children embody their own identities or respond to those of other children. With a knowledge of history, particularly a history of harm and oppression, students may not adopt race or gender language and images as blindly or as comfortably as they might have before. Thereby, they make vulnerable the reach and potency of the historically developed norms underlying these words and representations. The students could jeopardize the ability of these norms to grasp them and forcefully shape their bodies and language. Moreover, aligned with one of Butler's goals I depicted in chapter 4, some students may become capable of exploiting the fact that these norms never can fully grasp anyone and that, even when normative words and images bear a history of force, the norms are never entirely effective. Finally, insofar as "part of the work of whiteness involves generating norms—that is, making things seem or appear natural and timeless so that people accept situations, as well as particular ideologies, without ever questioning their socially and politically constructed nature," teaching about the historical presence and harms of such norms can work to tear down this privileged position of whiteness.[16]

ENVIRONMENTAL INFLUENCES ON GENDER AND RACE

Building from their historical investigation of race and gender, teachers in the classrooms I envision may begin to focus on habits by assisting students in identifying and understanding aspects of their current environments that impact their lives as raced and gendered. Teachers should also help students identify problematic aspects of race and gender or poor relations between races and genders. Because not all people experience the environment in the same way, all students may not experience a seemingly identical situation as problematic. So while all students live in a racist world, for example, not all will experience it as such. Some who live in racially homogeneous areas may not be fully aware of racial inequalities, while others who are well served by racial oppression may not be cognizant of it or may underestimate its injurious capacities. Still others may deny the existence of inequalities, while others will recognize them but see no problem with them. Some contemporary schools may also downplay or deny the existence of racism within their walls, perhaps by proclaiming that their policies and classroom leaders are "color blind." Such institutional statements and philosophies may lead to or support student beliefs (especially those of white students) that racism is not a problem within their school walls, while it may actually be quite rampant. When guided by such claims, teachers too may have difficulty identifying the more implicit forms of racism that often lie hidden within the curriculum or even within the small, mundane activities of the classroom.

Nonetheless, I am hopeful that some teachers can help students become aware of the environmental influences on their gender and racial habits so that they can understand how they are led to act in certain ways and any inherent limitations therein. One way in which students could learn about their own habits as well as those culturally identified as raced or gendered is through the analysis of popular culture. Classes might study movies, comedians, song lyrics, and other popular formats that depict races and genders to identify which habits, such as ways of walking, deference to authority figures, or proclivities toward certain activities, are popularly perceived to demarcate race and gender. Media programs that particularly accentuate and poke fun at these habits, such as *Malibu's Most Wanted*, *Napoleon Dynamite*, *White Chicks*, or *Will & Grace*, may be especially helpful for bringing the socially defined aspects of raced and gendered life both into consciousness and into question. Students will likely discover that they adopt or replicate many of these habits themselves.

Habits acquire significance because of environmental conditions.[17] When environmental conditions, including the images of magazines or popular stories, emphasize certain aspects of living as pertinent to defining race or gender, these habits acquire significance. One way of changing habits is to alter the conditions that produce and effect them.[18] In order to do so, schools should create conditions that downplay or contest certain habits traditionally or problematically used to define race or gender, thereby opening up the boundaries of appropriate race and gender. For example, I recall many units on dance within my K–12 physical education classes in the late 1980s and early 1990s. There, I and other girls learned larger standards of gender deference and power inequality through the molding of our bodies. We were shown how to wait politely for boys to ask us to dance and how to curtsy. We were praised for relinquishing control and allowing the boys to take the lead. Indeed, boys seemed to select us as partners in part because of our mastery of these skills but also because of other feminized traits, including our beauty or popularity. These classroom conditions concretized gendered norms by sculpting our bodily movements and activities. A physical education class aimed at downplaying or contesting these habits might encourage all children to take turns at leading on the dance floor regardless of gender. Moreover, the teacher might encourage same-sex dancing pairs, invite groups to dance together, or suggest that a dancer of any gender may initiate the dance.

It is by virtue of the very nature of habits as providing a deeply embedded sense of self and socialization that some students will likely cling to certain habits as representative of traditionally defined races or genders. While a teacher would be hard pressed to undo many years of cultural conditioning to see and understand race or gender in these terms within a nine-month school year, a teacher may try engaging the student in considering why these habits should continue to define race/gender or why race/gender are even necessary categories themselves. Students can be pushed to consider why they need these identity categories, whose interests they serve, and how their self-identities revolve around a certain set of fixed habits. These discussions may persuade the students to at least question their views and, through such inquiry, their performance of the habits being debated.

Even students who do become proficient at flexibly adapting themselves in the classroom may confront difficult situations both in and outside the classroom that risk reinstating past bad habits. Leaving a classroom environment that is supportive of difference and entering a racist and sexist world may invite transactions that reinstitute problematic ways of being. Or the traditional institutional practices of the school may actually be resistant to the change that stems from the flexible habits of individuals and try to overturn it. It is my hope that when new flexible habits prove fruitful in the classroom and teachers attune students to this fact, children will continue to seek and work toward such fruitfulness even when outside the classroom. Admittedly, this will require a strong foundation for such practices to be initially established in the classroom, and not all students will be successful when leaving that safe space.

I contend that a focus on environmental conditions effecting habits will help guide students in dealing with knotty circumstances of identity they may encounter. Or, in Dewey's words, "instruction in what to do next can never come from an infinite goal, which for us is bound to be empty. It can be derived only from study of the deficiencies, irregularities and possibilities of the actual situation."[19] Knowledge and investigation of the intricacies of one's environment can productively steer students, especially as they deal with new impulses and change of habit. Such activities can guide students in forming flexible habits that are themselves closely attuned to present contexts. An understanding of how present environments impact one's race and gender may help one best decide how to engage a current situation or make changes for the future. To quote Dewey further,

> In order that education of the young be efficacious in inducing an improved society, it is not necessary for adults to have a formulated definite ideal of some better state. An educational enterprise conducted in this spirit would probably end merely in substituting one rigidity for another. What is necessary is that habits be formed which are more intelligent, more sensitively percipient, more informed with foresight, more aware of what they are about, more direct and sincere, more flexibly responsive than those now current. Then they will meet their own problems and propose their own improvements.[20]

We see through these quotes from Dewey and the understanding emerging here that the focus is in the present context. A teacher should not have already reached a comprehensive vision of the good life she wants children to reach—an "infinite goal" that may include a detailed depiction of an end to racism or sexism. Instead, emphasis should be on developing flexible habits that allow children to enact the best life possible within the environmental conditions that vary from one moment to the next. As noted by other scholars of race and schooling, "social justice educators cannot proceed as if they already know exactly what antiracism is and what needs to be done to eradicate racism."[21] Antiracism—or what "qualifies" as antiracism—will change. It is always context specific, and teachers must emphasize this as they equip their students to best deal with current circumstances and fight against the racism within them. Certainly, however, teachers can uphold certain general goals, as I do, of effective communication, just consideration for the well-being of others, democratic participation in the leadership of a group, and the like. In the next section, I explain how pragmatic criteria can be used to assess student subversions, alterations, and other events. Even these goals and criteria, however, must be kept broad and open to critique.

FLEXIBLE HABITS AND NORMATIVE CHANGE

Much like those critics I described in chapter 4 who criticized Butler for not providing a detailed account of assessing change, I anticipate that some might raise similar concerns with my apparent valorization of flexibility without normative guidelines for evaluation. Some critics might ask, "Is flexible habit still a good thing if the habits taken up are bad?" Insofar as flexible habit is viewed as change in habit, the possibility that the new habit adopted is "bad" (generally meaning unethical, not good for one's well-being, or rigid) exists. Important to this adoption, however, is the process of change, which for me is one that has built-in pragmatic standards and is itself a process typically nurtured by leaders in an educational community. Flexible habit is most often guided by intelligent inquiry. It is this reflective process described in chapter 5, with its experimental nature and goals of fruitful living, that prevents new habits from being bad or at least from being bad for long. If the new habit does not prove to promote growth and well-being for the individual and for those surrounding him or her, the flexible habit is reworked, thereby preventing bad habits from sticking.[22]

Other critics might ask, "Are flexible habits good simply because they continually change?" My determination that flexible habits are good, while appreciative of the value of ongoing change, is centered on pragmatic justifications of good living, including the achievement of democracy, growth, successful leading, and fruitful transaction with the environment. Admittedly, these normative guidelines are rather open ended and lack definitive content. And they are almost always wrapped up in systems of power, as Butler warned previously.

Nussbaum faults Butler for not upholding a thoroughgoing normative vision that can guide and assess political change. Insofar as I adopt the normative views of Deweyan pragmatism, which is focused on present context, I, too, cannot offer a comprehensive normative vision that can be laid out once and for all. I can, however, use a pragmatic notion of flourishing and truth as what works to determine which changes are good and to have a sense for the direction in which change should occur. Pragmatists believe ideas become true insofar as they "work" for us, profitably combine our experiences, and lead us to further experiences that satisfy our needs. Pragmatists, like William James and Dewey, are concerned with the concrete differences in our lived experiences that an idea's being true will make. Pragmatic truth is "an expression of the anticipated or actual successful completing of a worthwhile leading."[23] Truth is something that occurs when the goals of human flourishing are satisfied, at least temporarily.

Insofar as habits are not ideas but rather the means by which they are formed and carried out, habits can be similarly assessed. As we try out new habits, we can strive to locate those that "work" for us.[24] The criteria of truth and flourishing, then, can be used to evaluate whether a change of habit has been beneficial or harmful. Built into these criteria is consideration of the well-being of others, for successful leading through experiences necessarily requires working and communicating with others. Determination of which habits to change or adopt through inquiry would also take into account how the new habit would fruitfully lead the individual and his or her community. While not a comprehensive vision of the good life, certain norms of democracy, equality, and just communication are entailed both in these deliberations and in their goals. These criteria can also be used by schools to determine which habits should be flexible and which should not. Schools should consider which habits might better serve their students and democracy when more flexible. I believe it is likely the case that school leaders would conclude that certain educational habits, like the training of handwriting, work well when established rigidly and uniformly for all, while they may also conclude that inhabiting one's race more flexibly may help tear down some of the fear and distrust between racial groups that prevents democracy from flourishing.

Importantly, pragmatic assessments are always contextual and may change from one case to the next, depending on the needs of the environment and the people involved in the situation. Moreover, in order to ensure flourishing for

all, these assessments must also overtly ask, "What works *for whom*?" or
"*Whose* needs?" While Nussbaum claims that norms like equality need to be
articulated to guide political activity, I suggest not that they must be articulated but that they need to be experienced at the level of coordinated habits in
order for them to be sought and maintained. Such embodied experience of
norms suggests a more active role for the body in crafting and responding to
its own conditions.[25]

Butler acknowledges some goods she wants to achieve through radical democracy and the exploration of discursive possibility. I contend that these
goods become significant and moral and thereby nonindividualistic when
they become meaningful. This occurs when they begin to operate at the embodied level of intelligent habit. Dewey describes the process of aligning normative assessments with our habits and with our communal learning activities. He says we should

> identify the sought for good with the meaning of our impulse and our habits, and
> the specific *moral* good or virtue with *learning* this meaning, a learning that
> takes us back not into an isolated self but out into the open-air world of objects
> and social ties, terminating in an increment of present significance.[26]

This normative element can be made more clear and meaningful when it is
openly shared and discussed in educational settings. Additionally, when students contextually see and experience the tentative normative visions and
standards of assessment, they are likely to have a motivation for questioning
and reworking problematic social structures. Because Butler's political project of resignification lacks this pragmatic justification and open exploration,
it is not apparent that students would be motivated to protest or purposively
resignify problematic identities or other power structures that constitute them.

FLEXIBLE HABITS AND AGENCY

Foucault describes power in a way that is particularly noteworthy for my interests here:

> In thinking of the mechanisms of power, I am thinking . . . of its capillary form
> of existence, the point where power reaches into the very grain of individuals,
> touches their bodies and inserts itself into their actions and attitudes, their dis-
> courses, learning processes and everyday lives.[27]

Power certainly resides within our habits. But power not only reaches into
habits—these everyday aspects of embodied living—but also operates through

them. I want to suggest that political agency and political efficacy stem from habits and is magnified through the development and use of flexible habits.

My notion of flexible habit is closely tied to the conception of agency that arises from the work of Dewey and Butler. Flexible habits entail a propensity for change and sensitivity to resistance that supports and invites acts of corporeal and linguistic insubordination. They target and cultivate a likelihood and a possibility that seems to occur most often unpredictably for Butler. And while still retaining the potential for signifying in unexpected ways and with unintended effects, the process of inquiry and the role of the classroom can make political acts more intelligent, with effects that are seen, foreseen, and experienced. Thereby, a more just motivation for and assessment of political agency and activity is offered. More than just a chance resignification, flexible habits entail an active confrontation with the symbolic realm, where conflicts among values and the failures of ideals are targeted and exposed through an intelligent, educational process.

Agency is often enhanced and educational goals are achieved through practicing the process of changing and developing new habits. This activity is well suited for the classroom. Educational situations may be constructed that raise student awareness of their habits and the ways in which their habits might be implicated in problems, including tendencies to disconnect from students different from oneself, rigidity in traversing a changing world, and failures to communicate with others. Teachers should aid students in the process of intelligent reflection and attune them to their actions and corresponding consequences. Within classrooms, students can engage in activities that link people, like work and civics, thereby helping students to understand the ways their activities affect others, their potential for agency, and their ability to produce political change.

The notion of agency emerging here, as informed by both Dewey and Butler, suggests an element of skill in traversing problems well. That skill is the intelligent enactment of flexible habits, including the use of and response to speech. As a skill, it is an ability that can—and perhaps should—be cultivated in the chief social institution of skill building: schools. Without making the effects of political agency through mass teaching clichés or commodities,[28] developing flexible habits can provide resources for countering social problems. Dewey thought that democratic action required having certain tools, tools developed through education. Flexible habits provide these tools of democratic agency.

As a skill or tool, agency via flexible habits is something that is reflected on and intentionally used. In light of my comments earlier, these elements seem to contradict performativity and iterability as described by Butler, especially given that Butler does not allow self-reflexivity because one cannot get outside of power to reflect.[29] Following Butler's critic Veronica Vasterling, I believe that political change can still happen in the way Butler describes, yet agents can be reflective and intentional—where this sense of intention is not a humanist notion of having complete control over the world.[30] Moreover, their political effectiveness is most likely strengthened insofar as these are active, intelligent activities as opposed to Butler's more passive sense of agency as a capacity. Schools could well be tasked with cultivating and refining reflection primarily within the context of problematic situations and reworking habits. Students can learn how to reflect within and because of power, and they can learn how their reflections on their activities helps ensure that change is positive.[31] They could also overtly discuss systems of oppression, constraints of identity, and the status of democratic living in order to guide student intention and goals.

While certainly facing many hindrances in the current educational climate, I do believe that classrooms can provide a space that supports and is sensitive to acts of subversion—a space where alternative ways of being are tested out and where political change is collectively forged. Following Butler, I am not suggesting that subjects (students) take up new identities here at random. Rather, the classroom should form a discourse where new or alternative meanings of race/gender are cultivated in ways that produce possibilities for new alternatives for students. Such a classroom would make resistance conceivable, possible, and meaningful. Indeed, such an institutional and social space could bring attention to flexible habits, for otherwise they might go unnoted. As institutions themselves struggle to determine which of students' habits should be flexible and which should not, overt discussion of the possibility and existence of flexible habits seems fitting. Schools could draw attention to the significance of flexible habits and ways in which others might respond to and join in with the changing habits of an individual student. Not only might teachers unite the acts of their individual students, but they also might teach students about and unite them with larger social efforts for change—revealing to students the power of social collaboration and the far-reaching effects of individual agency. Robert Westbrook, drawing on Dewey's own words, described this well in terms of Dewey's conception of politics as organized intelligence that analyzes social ends and works to secure them:

> Political activity in a democracy was in the broadest sense an educational enterprise, but this function did not rule out the exercise of power. True education was not "a cloistered withdrawal from the scene of action," for "there is no education when ideas and knowledge are not translated into emotion, interest, and volitions. There must be constant accompanying organization and direction or organized action and practical work. 'Ideas' must be linked to the practical situation, however, hurly-burly that is."[32]

Within each classroom, students could be guided through the process of inquiry at the level of both reflection and action. Teachers could encourage students (many of whom may be resistant to such activity) to investigate their subject positions and how they are implicated in the oppression of others or themselves. Through the teaching of history and language arts, students may learn about discursive and material traditions of violence and exclusion. They could learn about the force of injury that certain words and interpellations bear when cited in specific contexts and learn how to work against or rework those terms in ways that become affirmative. Students should become more aware of how they are constituted through interpellation and analyze moments in history where they and others have challenged or failed to fulfill interpellations, perhaps because of insubordinate acts or by virtue of the excess of their being that evades being pinned down into identity categories. More just and positive events of history can teach students "to appreciate the values of social life" and give them motivation to promote it in the present.[33] These types of teachings can raise student moral commitment to justice such that when privileged students learn of their complicity in injustice, they are more likely to be less comfortable with their privileged positions and change themselves. Of course, teachers must be careful not to romantically uphold the ideal of an individual "hero" student who can stand outside the situation and work against injustice.[34] For clearly, such voluntaristic activity would overlook Butler's account of subjugation and each individual's ongoing acts of complicity, if not outright injustice, therein. Moreover, such voluntarism overlooks the processes of habit conflict and problems with the environment that most often bring about habit change. Students cannot choose to abandon their identities, but some can invoke their agency to craft subversions of them and to replace elements of their privilege related habits with those that are more just or that disrupt the traditional category they represented. Crossroads between students may be forged during such activity.

Within schools, flexible habits could be targeted in ways that display the ambiguity and arbitrariness of identity. Insofar as apparently natural and fixed identity markers, such as gender and race, are actually habitual, flexible habits, as the ability to vary and resignify even these markers, can reveal that identity is never fully determined and is subject to construction. And communication, as a means and goal of changing habit, can assist students in making sense of and acting on this revealed fact. Teachers could help students understand themselves and envision their future relative to shifting identities that are open to critique.

Within all of her discussions of performativity and political agency, Butler almost never discusses the role of schools in enhancing agency or being a space where it plays out. And while Dewey does initially attribute significant influence of schools on developing agency, particularly in the context of cultivating democratic citizens, over time he grew less confident that schools could be the chief location of building political agency and democracy.[35] But certainly, however, given the notions of agency and flexible habits constructed here from both philosophers, schools with socially progressive agendas and support for opening up identities could be key places where students develop political agency and enact it in pursuit of social goals and justice. Even within schools that are not nearly so conducive to such undertakings, children may acquire some skills and inklings that may disrupt problems related to the stagnant sedimentation of the socially reproductive and therefore perpetually racist and sexist habitus.

CONFRONTING AND CHANGING HABIT

Bringing one's habits into explicit contact with those of someone different from oneself provides another opportunity for them to be challenged, changed, or confirmed. Philosopher of education Jim Garrison explains, "Habits are unconscious until something disrupts them. Dialoging across differences disrupts our habits of social interaction."[36] When talking, playing, or engaging in learning activities with those different from ourselves, our ordinary ways of being may falter and no longer allow us to act with ease. We may find ourselves fumbling over words or becoming self-conscious of our clumsy or inappropriate movements. In one elementary classroom, for example, several boys were forced to read a traditionally feminine book with a group of girls.[37] The boys found that they could not engage with the girls in the reading group or the feminine book in the ways they had traditionally been accustomed in terms of both their approach to reading and the way they discussed the book with classmates. They appeared to be both embarrassed and uncomfortable. Their initial handling of the situation entailed disruptive laughter and poking fun at the book and girls who enjoyed it. The problematic situation that arises in this case and others might provoke inquiry into the limitations of our past habits or our faulty assumptions about the habits of others. Indeed, it appears in the reading group example that the boys reworked their assumptions about girls' books and became more comfortable with performing gender differently through their interaction with the girls and their book. They eventually showed genuine interest in the story and fashioned new ways of participating in the group project to best facilitate their new environment of two genders. This change was due in large part to the fact that the boys' typical approach to reading did not work for this group or book, and the boys became curious about the girls' enthusiasm for the book and opened themselves to learning more about the book, the girls, and a different way of doing group work.

Classrooms that engage in this type of disruptive activity could make the habits *of* race and gender, as well as students' reactionary habits *to* race and gender difference, no longer routine but conscious and flexible. Thereby, they could become fluid and formed in light of future interactions across difference. One example of changing both one's habits *of* and *to* race worth mentioning is that of two young boys who come to create a friendship and a language. Dao (Chinese) entered his new school unable to speak English. He was quiet and unnoticed by most children and teachers who did not take the time to try to communicate with him.[38] Over time, Jason (Middle Eastern) took an interest in Dao and got to know him. They spent a great deal of time together, a considerable portion of which was devoted to imitating each other's activities and "bridging their ethnic and cultural differences."[39] Eventually, the boys mutually developed their own language—a blending of Chinese and English, with a few other inventions. Dao and Jason are observed struggling to communicate across their differences when their typical ways of speaking do not prove effective. They patiently and carefully study each others' actions and speech. They become aware of and try out each other's typical habits, some of which are directly related to race and language. They modify themselves accordingly so that they can reach an understanding of each other. They adjust both the ways in which they enact their own races and the patterns of speech related to them and the ways in which they typically interact with other children different from themselves. Ultimately, they are able to forge a new language within this space of embodied understanding. The ways in which they make themselves adaptable in this situation could be useful for other situations of encountering difference in the future as well.

Of course, these habit changing experiences could not entail a wholesale questioning of one's own habits because all of them cannot be brought out at once, nor are all habits easily called into consciousness. Some habits are deeply ingrained and are very difficult to change. A teacher skilled at crafting delicate learning opportunities may be able to draw out some of these most deeply held and often most problematically sedimented habits.[40] One way of doing this would be to encourage the student to inquire into what about herself is preserved when she changes during a learning experience or transactive encounter. Focusing the student on a specific race- or gender-related problem that she has experienced would be of use here, for it is in the most dangerous and problematic of lived situations when habits are often revealed. She can be challenged to identify those habits that so thoughtlessly constitute her identity—perhaps habits of prejudice that may be impeding her transactions with others and that she may be stubborn about bringing to the forefront in her transactions with them. For example, teacher Mica Pollock relates an intriguing exchange with Tina, one of her students:

> Tina, a self-described "black" student, was telling me one day that she had been accepted at "academic" Whitman but didn't "want to be in that environment" because it wasn't "black" enough. When I asked her to describe who has gone to Whitman from her middle school, she responded, "Filipino kids, and of course Chinese kids."[41]

Pollock, as a teacher, could guide Tina in considering what parts of her blackness were most fundamental or fixed and how these became clear through her visits to and consideration of different schools to attend. Coming to see which aspects of her blackness were not reconcilable with the nonblack environment she perceived at Whitman might help her understand how adhering to certain images of blackness or habits of race were inhibiting her options or narrowing her list of viable choices.[42] Stagnant ways of both habitually enacting and responding to race might then be brought to the fore.

Admittedly, this can be a highly difficult and risky introspection insofar as it makes our deeply rooted habits conscious and jeopardizes our very sense of self. One tool a teacher could use to aid this process would be to assist the student in viewing herself from without, perhaps by creating a hypothetical scenario for her to consider, urging her to describe how her actions may appear to a stranger, or by writing about her activities from the viewpoint of a news reporter. Approaching her situation from a third-person perspective may help unveil her most inflexible and deeply ingrained habits. Once rigid habits are called into view, students are more likely able to change how they are raced and gendered over time by replacing those stagnant habits, particularly if students discover that those habits are responsible for promoting sharp differentiations between genders or races and thereby limiting transaction. Pre-dating and differing considerably from both Butler and Dewey, this approach bears resemblance to Aristotle's approach to the habituation of character. Through dialogue and careful supervision, Aristotle believed that teachers should help students see the problematic patterns or weaknesses in their habits.[43]

For Dewey,

> The acquiring of new habits is due to an original plasticity of our natures: to our ability to vary responses till we find an appropriate and efficient way of acting. Routine habits, and habits that possess us instead of our possessing them, are habits which put an end to plasticity. They mark the close of power to vary.[44]

Butler explains that routine habits, regulated through repetition, form naturalized genders, races, and normative sexualities.[45] I contend, however, that dynamic habits of race and gender, while still allowing for continuity of identity, are more likely to prevent such sedimented formations whose naturalization often involves hierarchical categorization. Additionally and more in accord with Butler's view, specific habits of flexibility can be encouraged that vary those repetitions and thereby subvert the naturalized categories. Impulses, which are particularly supple in young children, typically deviate from or oppose standard repetition. These impulses can be used in the spur of the moment or "continuously and moderately" in the educational process to bring freshness to habit and to combat the routinization that entrenches the hierarchies Butler identifies.[46] And while Butler correctly warns that the precise content or method for how to challenge sedimented hierarchical structures cannot be identified, prescribed, or judged out of context, I believe that students can develop proclivities to change and subvert via flexible habits.[47]

Many of these predispositions can be developed in terms of habits of flexibility, that is, habits characterized by flexibility—the other sense of flexible habits I briefly described in chapter 5. While a good part of the school day is justifiably devoted to schooling students in rather uncreative skills, teachers can devote part of their time to crafting activities that support and reinforce student creativity, openness to new ideas, fantasy, playfulness, or theatrical inclinations. These habits may increase student likelihood and mastery of parody and subversion, which itself can provoke the reworking of bad habits or reveal identity-related problems. But they may also be the same types of traits that would make students more sensitive to some of their most deeply ingrained and problematic habits. They also may beneficially facilitate interaction across difference and experimentation in new ways of being. Cultivation of these particular habits should also be a central part of the pedagogy and curriculum I envision. Emphasizing habits of flexibility may be especially important when working with students for whom knowing or seeing the harmfulness of their bad habits still may not be enough to make them change. At least nurturing habits of flexibility can foster conditions for possibility so that opportunities for inquiry, change, or subversion may continue to open in the future.

I would also invite teachers to aid students in attending to their habits so that they will be able to recognize when their habits need to be altered or when the cultural structures influencing those habits (including in some cases those of the school itself) need to be challenged.[48] This can be a highly difficult task because some students who are members of dominant groups, such as the white boys on the racially divided British school playground described earlier, may not experience lack of communication or unjust interaction with members of oppressed groups as problematic. In fact, they may not even notice the problems of such relations at all. These situations have maintained their privilege for years and may not readily appear in need of being changed. In these instances, teachers need to effectively point out and explicate (without reinforcing or usurping) the experiences of the oppressed groups so as to bring them to light for the students of dominant backgrounds.[49] In Deweyan fashion, this is best done by creating a situation that reveals these problems to students through their own experience of them. Because habits cannot be changed directly, teachers must change those environmental conditions that, when disturbed, provoke indeterminate situations and ultimately change of habit.[50] This could entail moving a dominant white student from a desk surrounded by other whites to an area of the room populated by racial minorities, where he or she might experience exclusion and decreased attention and see his or her own racial peer group from a different perspective.[51] While it would be overly optimistic to think that simply putting students in racially mixed contexts would eliminate racism, such mixing from an early age has been effective in lessening overt racism in many cases.

Even though some hope does lie in enrolling kids in racially diverse schools from an early age, Jonathan Kozol has recently documented just how rampant resegregation currently is in America and how unlikely it is for the majority of students to currently occupy thoroughly racially integrated schools.[52] While everyone should be fighting to end resegregation, teachers must come up with coping strategies in the meantime. These may include developing an environment in the classroom that recognizes and appreciates diversity even in its physical absence and that dissuades from the development of racist habits.

The transactional exchange between individuals and environments leads to a mutual relationship between human and institutional habits. Because each affects the other, human habitual alteration may provoke change in institutions and vice versa. Charlene Haddock Seigfried notes,

> Institutions often appear to be impervious to change, but they are still complexes of habits and as such can be intelligently redirected. Truly radical change cannot be brought about merely through replacing formal structures, however, drastic as such substitutions are. Habits of thought and desire must also change, and this is best affected in young people who have not yet been fully imbued with established customs.[53]

Schools must be aware of the possibility that the very habits they develop within students may be used to subvert or challenge the ethos of the school. In this regard, while the school provides structure for forming flexible habits, the structure itself must be relatively flexible and revisable, dynamically prepared to work through changes in the future among its student body or the environment at large.

As transactionally reciprocal, changes in institutions may also provoke change in individuals. Indeed, changes in institutions, including their guiding beliefs and social goals, are an important part of supporting, enhancing, and extending a pedagogy based on flexible habits. Racism and sexism are composed of both individual and institutional habits that impact each other. Reworking these habits in social settings, perhaps under dynamic leaders or guided by new policies, may beneficially affect the habits of individuals.[54] While my project calls for a large part of transformation of identity and practices of inequality to begin with individual habits, this is certainly not the only way in which change can and should occur.

UNCOMFORTABILITY AND WHITENESS

While Dewey and many more recent philosophers and psychologists often prize the comfort and sense of self that stems from a stable identity, my focus on flexible habits suggests that it may be better for students to be made uncomfortable with their identities in some situations. Discomfort with the gender and racial habits they bring to the classroom may assist in bringing problematic habits into consciousness, igniting inquiry into them, and possibly aiding in altering them. I do not want to argue that this discomfort should be perpetually present insofar as this would jeopardize the ease of traversing the world that habits provide and would render habits so overly scrutinized that they would no longer function as habits at all. I do want to suggest that it is appropriate for students to be made uncomfortable at times and that they should be sensitive to discomfort as a feeling indicative of potential problems or a need to change.

Provoking students to see conflicts within their own raced and gendered habits can be educationally productive. While this activity can be directly taught in only a small handful of cases, it is more fruitful to usher students into situations that might reveal these problems. Teachers, on getting to know each individual student well and identifying some rigid habits of identity that impede their activities or interactions with others, can construct some of these situations. However, they must be true to life and meaningful rather than artificial and imposed. For only if they are seen as valid and arising from oneself are these situations capable of being transformed from indeterminate to problematic. Indeterminate situations are not cognitive, and the guttural sense that they are occurring may be unnoted or misread by students. Teachers can guide students in attuning to feelings of unrest or inklings of unease that may induce inquiry and thereby identify a problem to be redressed. For, in a Deweyan sense, "problems are not simply 'there' but emerge as a result of the identification of an indeterminate situation *as* being problematic, *as* being in need of inquiry."[55]

Whiteness

Whiteness, in particular, poses some interesting problems in terms of comfort. Whiteness can be understood as a position of privilege or perhaps as a collective name for the efforts of certain types of people to establish and maintain privilege. White privilege differs from other types of privileges in key ways. Some privileges are earned. A gifted athlete like Lance Armstrong, for example, may earn privileges of fame, including a special seat at his favorite restaurant or free racing shoes. Other privileges are given out indiscriminately to some people and are permissible because they are relatively inconsequential. Some factory workers, for example, may be granted a five-minute morning coffee break while others are not. White privilege, in contrast, entails receiving special benefits and advantages that are unearned and are awarded on the basis of one's race. In many cases, however, white privilege is not straightforward. In the instance of a poor white person, for example, the privileges accorded by race may be downplayed by the privileges denied by low social class. Nonetheless, the advantages conferred by white privilege are often significant. In some cases, the privileges awarded are goods, like respect in public settings or concern for one's well-being. These are privileges that would be had by all in a fully just society of fair distribution and recognition. Other privileges may authorize white people to perform certain acts that would be impermissible if done by those of another race, or they may exempt whites from certain burdensome or unpleasing activities. These privileges are problematic because they assign unearned power and positions of authority to whites. White privilege often operates as an unspoken social relation between people that favors whites and maintains or extends current racial inequalities or oppression.

While other privileges, including those related to class and religion, may intersect with or in some cases trump white privilege, I focus on white privilege because it is an important theoretical tool for understanding the perpetuation of racial dominance and often plays out through habits. Through the process of transaction, we can begin to see how white privilege is lived at the level of individuals yet both reinforces and is reinforced by the larger culture of white dominance. White racism and superiority then reside within both individuals and society. Whiteness and its privileges may take form as habits of comportment by carrying oneself with presumed entitlement, habits of perception by being oblivious to the impact of race on the lives of minorities, or as predispositions to make certain assumptions about others by grouping them into stereotypes while seeing whites as unique individuals. There is no comprehensive definition of whiteness, but we can see that whites generally tend to exhibit certain patterns of habits, even though those habits vary, depending on the context of the individual enacting them.

Comfort with the status of privilege in light of white complicity or outright participation in oppression is surely problematic. Cris Mayo argues that whiteness has been a way of having "certainty and self-protection" when it comes to securing privileges and being untroubled by knotty issues of race.[56] Unfortunately, many white students do not feel troubled enough by the link between privilege and oppression to work against it. In fact, many, if not the majority, do not even recognize their privilege.[57] Whiteness as privilege is a hard habit to break because it often goes undetected by whites or because it simply does not pay to be antiracist or nonwhite. Even as whites reap the rewards of unjustified white privilege, they may do so unknowingly, they may feel as though they have earned the benefits on the basis of nonrace criteria, or they may enjoy the advantages to such an extent that they do not feel motivated to question them. When we acknowledge the staying force of bad habits as well as the attractive benefits of institutions that privilege whites, we can see why many white individuals maintain their habits and positions of privilege. The possibility of achieving racial equality and harmony depends on all individuals recognizing their specific links to white privilege; acknowledging how their habits maintain, benefit, or suffer from such a system; putting an end to inaction; and holding individuals responsible for the quality of their efforts to eliminate white privilege. As the form of racism has changed over the years from overt white supremacy to more subtle white privilege, our habits underlie those changes and will continue to be a key part of future progress toward eliminating racial discord and inequality.

Whiteness is often the unnamed norm against which other races are measured. One of the few cases in which whiteness is named is when it is used (often by whites themselves) in phrases such as "white trash" to differentiate certain sub(par)groups of whites from those of greater privilege. An even more blatant phrase, "poor white trash," is also used. It overtly points out how this population differs from the white norm of financial security or wealth.[58] To some extent and in some cases, revealing whiteness, privilege, and oppression can help work against the problems of whiteness and can disclose to white and nonwhite children problems with their racial position that might otherwise have gone unnoted.

Certainly, the positions of whites are often noted in many cases by minority students. Educational researcher Amanda Lewis shares one particularly telling example:

> One day while driving three African American boys (Darnell, Malik, and Thompson) to a school to watch a basketball game, I explained to them that I had never been to that school but my understanding was that it was at a pretty "fancy" place. Malik assured me that it wouldn't be a problem: "Don't worry, Ms. Lewis, Darnell knows how to talk white." Darnell proceeded through a series of impersonations

that the other boys practiced imitating in between their fits of giggles. Darnell's impersonations included among others, a haughty, refined accent ("Get my slippers, Geoffrey"), a hillbilly voice ("Whaddya say, Billy?"), a sort of military tone ("All right, son"), and a repressed sounding teacher ("Okay, class"). This particular incident provided a glimpse of two clear understandings about whiteness. Not only was my signal about class status ("fancy") immediately read as a racial signifier, but the boys' impersonations were almost all voices of authority giving instructions to subordinates. In interviews, these and other boys talked about whites as people who were sometimes racist, often mysterious, and definitely powerful.[59]

These boys were clearly aware not only of differences between whites but also of the various senses of privilege that underlie each.

The protected parade of privilege can be disrupted in part by rendering whiteness visible, often through exposing or troubling the meanings of performing whiteness as well as the comfort level that underlies them and the cultural conditions that support them. I agree with Megan Boler, who suggests that these revealing classroom exercises should be challenging. Sounding much like my sense of stagnant habits of privilege, Boler says that "inscribed habits of emotional inattention" can be revealed through the discomfort that challenges one's typical views.[60]

Boler rightly suggests that teachers must be prepared to handle students' responses to these revealing teachings with compassion and, I would add, patience. Students must often be carefully guided through the experiences of denial, fear, anger, and shame that may arise from exploring privilege, oppression, and complicity. Problematically, these pedagogical exercises often lead white students to be defensive, proclaiming that they, unlike their other white peers or previous generations, are not racist. Some students can become quite hostile, while others deny that racial inequalities even exist in the first place. Still others, if they decide that they want to work against racism, tend to engage in conversations that problematically recenter their position of authority and power even as they claim to want to contest it.[61] They may problematically adopt a mentality of heroism where they believe that have volunteered to valiantly acknowledge their privilege and fight against it. This heroism emphasizes the actions of the whites and often of individuals in particular rather than the lengthy efforts of minority groups to bring these issues to the fore and to push whites into considering them.[62]

A Pedagogy of Discomfort

Simply revealing whiteness as privilege may not be enough. White students need to be made uncomfortable with their position as such and with their habits that maintain it—including dominance within cross-racial dialogue, commanding presence when confronting those different from themselves, carrying themselves with presumed entitlement, and general ease of traversing shopping centers, police stations, political circles, and other racially prejudiced areas. For example, a key teaching moment rises and passes during the classroom art project described at the beginning of chapter 3. The teacher, Debi, instructs the children to choose a paint that matches their skins in order to paint a representation of their hands. Corinne, a young African/white biracial girl, insists against the teacher's instructions that she use two paints, one dark brown and one pale brown. She paints two differently colored hand prints and writes her name between them, exclaiming, "Perfect!" A black girl, Taleshia, chooses a pale pink paint. When the teacher puts the paint up to her arm to show that they do not match, Taleshia insists on the pink, showing that the rosy palms of her hands to Debi. Visibly upset, a white girl, Robin, insists that pink is the wrong color for Taleshia and begins to shout at her, as does another white girl. All the white children selected a single shade of peach to represent their skins. In this case, Debi has the opportunity to guide the children in a discussion of how skin color corresponds to racial identity and how certain privileged interests are served when color is narrowly understood. Taleshia has already troubled color identification with her selection of pink, and two other African American children have introduced complexity in their color selection as well. If the children were mature enough to handle such a discussion, the teacher might push the children to consider why the white children—and Robin in particular—adhere so strongly to a narrow conception of whiteness and color acceptability. The teacher should make Robin uncomfortable with her commanding determination of which colors are appropriate and how she conveys this through intimidating and authoritative shouting. Instead, Debi's narrow interpretation of the assignment itself prevents a variety of colorful interpretations from being chosen and reinforces a limited understanding of race and perpetuation of white dominance.[63]

More than just students from the dominant group must be nudged out of comfort zones, however. Nonwhite students have likely experienced hegemony that has shaped their own values and views of complicity and privilege. These students also should be guided through the revelation of these hegemonic effects and in the sense of discomfort that comes with this process. Admittedly, such activities are politically controversial, and teachers who engage in them must either have the support of the larger school system or be willing to take educational risks and be prepared to offer a rationale for them, perhaps one similar to that offered within these pages.

Being pulled into a space of discomfort can also spark an array of emotional responses among students of all races and genders. Some students may feel angry and defensive as they sense that their identities are in jeopardy or feel as though they are being attacked. Whites or men may feel that they are unfairly being labeled racist or sexist and may effectively reestablish their position of authority even as they seemingly benignly try to defuse or divert the situation by claiming that they are color blind, proclaiming their friendship with kids from other races or genders, describing instances of their own victimization, or citing samples of minorities or women who have been successful as evidence that racism and sexism have receded. Other students may be angry when truly seeing and feeling racial injustices for the first time. Others may feel guilty on discovering their complicity or participation in those injustices. Some students may withdraw from the conversation, sensing its difficulty or perhaps trying to avoid confrontation. This is especially the case for many young women, particularly those from the Midwest or South, who have been taught to avoid confrontation.[64] Still others may feel that the discussion is inappropriate insofar as it questions the way society runs and they sense that this is either dangerous or a waste of time. Engaging in a pedagogy of discomfort requires facing and investigating these emotional responses as markers of our habits, signs of the ways we experience racism/sexism, or, in some cases, resistance to change. This takes courage on the part of both students and teachers. It requires a brave willingness to push oneself and to get at the very heart of our races and genders. Teachers should encourage and praise those who are willing to take such bold steps and delicately guide those who may be less daring or less equipped to handle emotional, intellectual, and physical strain.

While whiteness cannot be erased, in many instances it can be made visible and its dominating power disrupted. Moreover, skilled and patient teachers can teach students (whites in particular) about their link to oppression in ways that can develop and sustain a guttural and conscious sense of discomfort. This discomfort can be harnessed through the change of habit to transform oneself until ways of being that are more just are reached. Unlike traditional forms of multicultural education that shore up and simplistically celebrate racial groups or more recent curricula that paralyzingly induce white guilt, I am calling for an educational approach where whiteness can be transformed into something that is positive and counterhegemonic and enables whites "to travel in and out of various racial/ethnic circles with confidence and empathy."[65] Rather than producing a fixed identity, then, as past and current approaches have done, this new identity is dynamic and will continue to transition as the world around it, including forms of racism, changes. To achieve this new white identity, pedagogies of discomfort "can decenter students' identities and ideologies so as to help them connect past injustices not only with how such injustices continue in the present; also, it can get them to understand that changes in the present can be made based on knowledge of the past. In this sense, students gain a sense of hope that they can contribute to a better world by living their whiteness progressively."[66]

I support two pedagogical approaches that Boler offers to help guide students through these difficult transformations: the teaching about the costs of whiteness to those who benefit from it[67] and the teaching of personal narratives of those who have recognized their complicity and joined with others in antiracist efforts.[68] These approaches may help white students better understand the problems of the privileged position and also provide them with a sense of how they might go about making change in the world in a moment of discomfort that might otherwise feel debilitating. Discussing the unfairness of privileges awarded due to whiteness may reveal the already precarious nature of whiteness and make white students uncomfortable with not having truly earned all their advantages.[69] The narratives, in particular, may offer students a model to follow or at least certain steps that can help them figure out where to go from here. Despite the potential benefits from these suggestions, it is imperative that we recognize how the habitual nature of performing whiteness may prevent them from being effective. To the extent that habits are unconscious, providing rational arguments or narratives about the shortcomings of whiteness will likely not be enough to cause problematic habits of whiteness to change. Because of this, change must be focused primarily at the level of everyday practice and operation of whiteness—at the taken-for-granted aspects of doing whiteness. Tools such as the ones Boler offers can supplement or prod reflection into those unconscious ways of being.

Uncomfortability also plays an interesting role in discussions of identity within the medical and psychological fields. Currently, one major symptom of gender identity disorder is being uncomfortable in one's gender.[70] My notion of flexible habits builds from a sense of discomfort as essential to improving identities in the present and possibly deteriorating them in the long run. This is especially true in the case of whiteness. Because of the key role of uncomfortablility, the definition of identity disorder is rendered nonsensical. To feel uncomfortable is not a disorder at all but a potentially productive state of unease that provokes transformation and possibly improves relations between people of different identities if not rewardingly changing the initial identity as well.

PRIVILEGED OVERSIGHT OF FLEXIBILITY

As I make calls here for flexibility and uncomfortability, I am compelled to consider my own history as a white woman and the privilege it carries. Throughout my elementary and high school days, I was largely able to navigate educational settings with ease and was able to do so while comfortably adhering to my whiteness. By closely analyzing events in my own classroom now and in those depicted within these pages that show signs of flexible habits as well as rampant problems of racism, I have come to see how my past rigid racial habits have participated in harm and oppression and how they have limited my own growth and experiences. With this realization and an appreciation for the efforts many students have already put forth in classrooms across the globe, I am now led to call for flexible habits in others—white and nonwhite. While a relatively recent development for me, a closer look at several classroom events suggests that many minority students have already been enacting some aspects of flexible habits that I did not notice in my earlier days of studying and participating in schooling. Moreover, these flexible identities also typically go unrecognized by schools, which continue to maintain an "official" version of race and gender that define identities as though all children fall easily into one discrete category or another.[71]

Peshkin, for example, shares the story of a multiracial boy who describes his raced activities as the setting around him changes:

> Sometimes I have to say "I be going, yeah, what about it." I have to talk that way so I don't get talked about and beat up. Like, say, I go downtown. If I go there talking like I am now [to me], they, you know, will just stare at me saying. "Look at that nigger trying to act white." When I'm around them I'm going, "Yeah, what's up man? You know, what it is. How it is." Then I go around whites and say, "Yeah, hello." Half the time I just walk normal black, but when I get around, you known, like my all-black hoodlum friends—well, they aren't friends of mine, I just known them—I just kick back. "What's up, man," and I dip. I dip. The old term for it was the quote "pimp walk." That means, like, to walk laid back, to one side, and you dip. That's weird because I be going, "Dang, I gotta go through all these changes just to fit in." Like my best friend, he say, "Warren, are you black or are you white?" I change, others change also, but they don't notice it because I don't tell them. Around different people, you have to act, you know, a different way.[72]

Warren has learned to vary the way he acts, speaks, and walks when he encounters different racial peer groups. He has learned to do this so that he can have multiple groups of friends as well as for his own protection. His habits flexibly adapt to ensure better transaction with those around him, and he has engaged in inquiry into how and when his habits should change. He is already enacting many of the key aspects of flexible habits and is doing so in ways that juxtapose his racial ambiguity with his citations of racially defined habits. This has raised the eyebrows of his friend and could be a good start on the path toward breaking down racial walls as a whole.

At another school, the continually shifting habits of the minority students, especially their patterns and manners of speech, struck one educational researcher and urged her to see the inadequacies of racial classification:

Student life at Columbus was always inordinately complicated, and so it often seemed that placing "racial" boundaries on Columbus students was an inherently inaccurate exercise. At Columbus, a "Filipino" student speaking Tagalog to a friend at one moment might call him "homie" the next, just as a "Latino" student might switch from speaking rapid Spanish to chanting rhythmic English rap lyrics under his breath.[73]

I suspect that my own prior obliviousness to the flexibility of Warren and these racially diverse Columbus High School students may be similarly shared by others whose comfortable positions of privilege have not demanded these continual changes. The beginnings of antiracist pedagogies, then, may already be alive and well among minority populations. I am not suggesting through this book that I created this solution on my own but rather highlighting these two examples as well as several instances depicted earlier in this book to show that this pedagogy of flexible habits arises not only theoretically out of Dewey and Butler but also out of the activities of some minorities. I am honoring their efforts by bearing the responsibility of illustrating and disseminating them among other people and especially among privileged whites who are, in many ways, most responsible for changing their bad habits in order to bring about an end to racism.

Efforts to end racism and sexism will require different habits particular to dominant and nondominant groups to be changed. Stagnant habits of whiteness that are related to comfortability with privilege, entitlement, and rugged individualism certainly require reworking among many whites, while masculine habits entailing dominance, authoritarianism, and supremacy must be addressed by many males. Minority populations also have a fair share of troubling bad habits that should also be subject to inquiry and change, though they tend to differ considerably in nature from those of members of dominant groups. In some cases, their problematic habits have been internalized through hegemony and actually perpetuate or excuse their own oppression. All groups can benefit from cultivating flexible habits that do not become problematically sedimented in many of the ways that these habits related to race and gender superiority have become. Acknowledging and modeling the struggles many minority people have already made in this direction can be one important beginning step in this process.

IDENTITY DECONSTRUCTION

Over the past few decades, many educational theorists and practitioners have championed the importance of building identities within children. Some have argued within the context of social justice education that certain identities need to be strengthened (such as providing a firmer foundation for whiteness since many whites do not have a sense of cultural connection and are then unable to understand the racial identities and cultural traditions of differently raced peoples) or changed and affirmed anew (such as changing whiteness from an identity of privilege to one of antiracist traits). Relatively few have called for an opposing approach to education: identity deconstruction. Insofar as my project of flexible habits adopts the political goals of Butler and the fluidity of Dewey, it is in the direction of deconstruction that my project turns. I am led in Butlerian spirit to ask, How can the constructed nature of racial and gender identity be used for subversion?[74] If a classroom has historically been a place where identities are constructed and solidified, might we rework it as a place where the constructions are constantly being done and undone? Might we target the act of construction itself to subvert its product? To the extent that identities are constructed through the cultivation of certain raced and gendered habits, I propose that teachers in the classrooms I envision should target this construction in ways that question the appropriateness of certain rigid habits and the larger identities they imply.

Classroom deconstruction has the capacity to reveal the violent and exclusionary act of identity construction by exposing the inability of identity categories to be fully inclusive as well as the detrimental implications of exclusionary groupings. Teachers could guide students through critical analysis of media, educational materials, and current events. They can highlight aspects of these materials that define directly or indirectly the boundaries of race and gender. A class might, for example, consider a recent public policy on marriage rights, questioning who receives these rights by the way gendered parties are defined. Or an elementary class might list the traits and activities of "good little girls" in fairy tales. Often these classroom activities will entail assisting students in seeing which people are excluded from these definitions. Recall the exercise of finding photos that match one's identity categories. The teacher could have better crafted her lesson by engaging in these types of questions about exclusion rather than enforcing boundaries by making children adhere to her visions of races and genders.

It can be quite difficult to identify who is excluded, for, as I described in chapter 4 on Butler's work, these people may not even be recognizable because they do not conform to the standards with which we recognize and engage others. Students can be exposed to bodies, like those of hermaphrodites, and habitual activities, like cross-dressing, that are often viewed as strange and unusual if they receive any attention at all from the general public. While careful not to make them spectacles or to label them as bad, this practice can denaturalize identity categories and reveal their exclusionary practices. Additionally, while the teacher cannot fully know what is foreclosed in a way that enables him or her to teach students to speak on the borders of foreclosure, the teacher can draw attention to those moments when students or educational materials do push the borders of linguistic acceptability. Thereby, teachers can accentuate both the existence of these borders and the possibility as well as current existence of those who lie outside of them.

By emphasizing the possibility and existence of alternative ways of being, the teacher could work to reveal that the dominant forms are not natural or original. Moreover, in advanced classrooms, teachers can guide students in considering how the definitions of naturalness protect the interests of certain privileged groups and how construction of these definitions and the identities they signify can be done differently. Boldt provocatively suggests that, when norms of gender are no longer seen as natural, the traditional blame can no longer be placed on a "gender identity disorder" child for not upholding his or her appropriate gender. Instead, the blame shifts, and the norms of gender are seen as failing the student.[75] Ideally, I would hope that the shortcomings of normative visions of genders themselves would then also be questioned. We see a raced case of this blame in the speech of the resigning Samoan club president. There, Tuli suffers from the blame others assign and her own sense of inadequacies of fulfilling the raced norm of Samoanness. Were this norm to be seen by the students as nonnatural and problematic, the frustrations of Tuli and her peers might better be directed at dissecting the racial norm itself insofar as it limits the ways that Tuli and others like her can behave. This shifting of blame also differs considerably from identity politics, where Tuli and other minorities must define themselves as different from dominant peoples yet also bear the burden of proving that they are worthy people who deserve rights and respect. This shift lifts the burden of responsibility from the shoulders of the minority or oppressed groups.

In the present context where rights claims often depend on definitive alliance with certain racial or gender groups and where people must uphold normative aspects of identity to achieve viability in the world, students must learn to inhabit racial and gendered subject positions. But they should do so while simultaneously learning to investigate and rework the exclusions that sustain them. This endeavor can push students from dominant groups into a fragile and uncomfortable space between a stagnant though viable past and a dangerous though exciting future full of new and more ethical ways of living. Teaching students within this delicate space will almost certainly entail guiding students through the process of relinquishing the coherence of themselves and their identities. Recognizing the complexities within themselves and the ways in which they exceed or do not fulfill the normative definitions of their races and genders may productively jeopardize this coherence. Thereby, the distance and differentiation instituted between people of difference because of a requirement to uphold coherence may be called into doubt, and students may begin to forge more just connections between themselves and others.[76]

Through creative writing, drama, and the reading of both fiction and non-fiction, students can engage in imaginative explorations that envision how race or gender could be (and often already are) lived differently. Additionally, they may fantasize about how they could respond in new or better ways to people of racial and gender difference—imagining how their habitual ways of responding to difference could be otherwise. Butler argues that fantasy is not merely cognitive play. Rather, "fantasy structures relationality, and it comes into play in the stylization of embodiment itself."[77] When this fantasy plays out on and through the body, subversion of stagnant coherent ways of being and other changes may occur.

Reconsider the chapter 5 introductory example of Renee, who contemplates whether her race is changing as the color of her arm changes with the spring sun. Here we see, even in a young child, the potential ways in which fantasy might shape the performance of raced bodies. Renee has already become curious about being black. The teacher's aide, Lynne, might have encouraged Renee to imagine being black or being raced in ways that complicated her tanning skin. Lynne might have introduced Renee to stories about black or biracial children. Renee's fantasies might have affected her raced habits, thereby changing her raced body or at least troubling it. Fantasy, then, "allows us to imagine ourselves and others otherwise. Fantasy is what establishes the possible in excess of the real; it points, it points elsewhere, and when it is embodied, it brings the elsewhere home."[78]

PROVOKING FLEXIBLE HABITS IN THE CLASSROOM

Rather than teaching children specific new habits of race and gender (which misunderstands how change occurs via habit), teachers need to work on making students' habits flexible and cultivating certain skills that provoke habit change. These skills include bodily awareness, questioning, sensitivity to the acts of others, reflexivity, and foresight, among others. In a paradoxical sense, one must secure these skills in order to live life flexibly—to fluidly take on new forms and to respond to those different from oneself with ease and adaptability. These skills provide the structure Dewey would likely argue is required to support the building and exploration of more flexible habits. In some ways, then, it may be more appropriate for schools to teach these skills in some of the entrenching ways that they teach skills like handwriting and spelling. Schools would be justified in doing so because these skills provide a basis for a multitude of social goods, including the ability to communicate with others well, the inclination to thoroughly investigate one's world, and self-knowledge that leads to more just interactions with others.

We cannot teach youth to suddenly enact their raced and gendered lives in new ways. We must begin with the habits they actively use and work at getting them to question and change those habits. Change comes about and through the habits themselves. Dewey claims that habits grow more varied and, I would add, more flexible when practiced.[79] If this is indeed the case, as I believe it is, teachers should aim to create scenarios where students have to employ habits of flexibility so that they gain practice and become mechanized in such responses. Play and art are sources for releasing impulses that might reconfigure habits so that they are enacted differently or for trying out new ways of being.[80] Educational sociologist Barrie Thorne, in her seminal work, *Gender Play*, aptly describes how children take play seriously and how play is a space where children learn to both enact and contest gender habits. Dewey also rightly emphasizes the importance of play.[81] For him, it is an activity in which one's interests and imagination are acted out in tactile engagement with the world. It is a complete activity, "the interplay of all of the child's powers, thoughts, and physical movements, in embodying, in a satisfying form, his own images and interests."[82] Free physical movement and interaction with tangible objects helps students learn about the consequences of their bodies and intentions as well as the physical laws of the world. Although social and physical control are important for Dewey, bodies should not be suppressed in classrooms. Rather, they should be schooled in how to behave significantly through play, communication, and meaning making.[83] Students should learn how to use their bodies as meaningful signifiers in order to perform the norms read on them consequentially. And they should learn how varying those performances through pursuing impulses and adapting their bodily habits opens up new ways of being and potentially pulls those norms into question.

Although in many cases limited by the demands of socializing children into socially acceptable ways of being, some classrooms can provide a space that supports and is sensitive to acts of playful subversion. Classrooms can be a space where alternatives can be tested out and where political change can be sought collectively. This type of setting makes resistance conceivable, possible, and meaningful. In many cases, students have already attempted to vary their habits or live differently, but their actions have gone unnoted or were scorned by others. Butler, as I noted in chapter 4, describes the life of a child who was born sexually ambiguous and was raised as a female. As she aged, she struggled to make sense of her gendered position somewhere between or beyond male and female. Some of her habits fell within the boundaries of each, but taken together, they rendered her gender incoherent. Her fellow students, unsure how to deal with the new ways of being she was exploring, threatened her one day when they discovered her standing to urinate in the school girls' bathroom. They claimed they would kill her if they caught her standing as boys do to urinate again.[84] In this case, the girl's behavior is seen as threatening and outside of acceptability, thereby shoring up or safeguarding the gendered norm.[85] This example shows that trying out new ways of being can be dangerous and that, beyond simply cultivating flexible habits, schools must create a space where these variations on being are welcomed and supported. To create this space, students must learn how to deal with confronting difference—how to make sense of it, how to respond to it, and how to reflect on their own lives in light of it. Rather than simply a multicultural curriculum that talks about difference, this requires students to be inextricably surrounded by difference—where different ways of being are continually being acted out, discussed, and explored in ways that do not reinforce the original norm.[86]

In order to be subversive, parody or variation of habit requires a setting that is sensitive to subversion. Without fully setting up or directing moments of student insurrection, teachers can highlight aspects of these moments so that they can be productively noticed by others and be detected in future situations. Moreover, in order to effect larger political change, the observers of such acts must learn how to analyze and, in some cases, join in them. Teachers can assist in this process. As I cautioned earlier, teachers must beware, however, that specific acts of insubordination are not taken up by students and repeated en masse by students in ways that render them clichés or are picked up for their commodity value. Rather, teachers should encourage the general adoption of flexible habits that provoked the insubordination in the first place.

In the case of Annette, the boisterous girl revered by the boys, her gender-crossing habits are supported by her male playmates. The boys carefully observe her gender-bending habits. These habits and her skills earn the respect of the boys and enable Annette to traverse the playing fields with ease. But this would not be the case if the boys did not notice Annette's habits and her ability to vary her gendered habits when in the presence of boys and sports. The boys, in turn, respond to Annette by diverging from the typical ways in which they interact with girls.[87] These boys diligently observe Annette, consider her unique gendered position, and alter themselves in light of her differences and her unique activities. They provide a space that supports her efforts and allows her to extend her activities beyond their small circle of friends to activities with other students both in and outside the classroom. Hopefully, over time, the habitual ways in which the boys enact their own genders and respond to other girls will also become more flexible. Honing observational skills is also an important part of a pedagogy aimed at opening up possibilities for identity because children who are good observers can see the variations of how their peers are raced and gendered, even if those variations are not acknowledged by the institution.

Children have already developed ways to resist in the classroom or in difficult situations of interacting with other children different from themselves. In some cases they may provoke laughter, while in others they may change the subject. But when student attention is directed toward habits, the aspects of these forms of resistance that stem from flexible habits can be magnified in beneficial ways. When students come to see similarities in subversive acts, they no longer appear disaggregated or otherwise nonconstructive. The acts of individuals can be united together to work toward larger efforts for social change so that the insurrections of individuals, while valuable in their own regard, actually change the original problems they confront rather than just parodying them but allowing them to stand. Teachers can help students identify these acts and shared frustrations they may have with identity or identity-based systems of oppression, then channel the efforts of students together. Of course, their individual acts would and should take varying forms, but the classrooms I envision can offer a space where students can be brought together in collaborative social action.

COMMUNICATION IN THE CLASSROOM

Important for fruitful transaction, flexible habits include flexibility in the ways in which one communicates with others. This includes how one speaks and listens in context-specific situations and relative to the habits of the other person with whom one is conversing. For Dewey, communication is "the establishment of cooperation in an activity in which there are partners, and in which the activity of each is modified and regulated by partnership."[88] Here, activity should be thought of as habits enacted by (and constitutive of) the body–mind of each participant. During activity, these habits are engaged in transaction and therefore open to being changed by and through one another. When both interlocutors come together with a shared concern for improving life's conditions and for communicating across their differences, it may be helpful but not necessary for them to consciously reflect on their habits. When their habits are characterized by openness or are held tentatively, the responses that they make to one another can be sufficient causes for each to modify their respective responses in turn, hence altering themselves to better achieve a fruitful transaction.[89] It follows that, for Dewey, communication "modifies the disposition of both the parties who partake in it."[90]

While a key aspect of communication is making meanings and experiences common, Sullivan offers an account of effective communication that is well aligned with my notion of changing habits. She says,

> The first step is akin to Socratic wisdom, or recognition of one's ignorance: one must realize that communication may not be taking place before one can begin to work toward it. One must realize that the habitual, nonreflective ways in which one understands another person may be contributing to a misunderstanding of her. In attending to bodies that are different from my own, communication with another becomes possible because acknowledging the ways in which a person's bodying, including its gestures, comportment, and style as well as appearance, is different from mine disturbs my assumption that I already understand its meaning. Rather than try to discover the familiar in another, one needs first to make strange that which seems familiar.[91]

This process of attending to and changing bodily habits when communicating offers an appropriate warning against the dangers of assuming commonality, a more thorough sense of effective communication, and some insight into situations where communication fails because of rigid or conflicting habits. Through her portrait, we begin to see the importance of modifying our own habits relative to the habits of our interlocutors and of modifying our habits on considering how they are interpreted by others. Teachers can construct lessons and activities that help children learn to astutely observe one another and constructively communicate their observations to each other in ways that allow each participant to beneficially alter his or her habits. While certainly not a formal or advanced approach to communicating in this way, we do see key aspects of this process occurring without the influence of a teacher in the example I described earlier of the two boys who create a shared language. As I described earlier, Dao and Jason perceptively observed one another and modified themselves in light of each others' habits. This enabled them to rework their customary ways of being and ultimately to forge a new system of communication. Teachers could benefit from highlighting and praising these activities as models for other students to follow.

Learning how to effectively communicate entails learning how one's embodied being affects and regulates that of another as they cooperate in meaning making. Butler has an especially keen sense of how speech acts issue from and affect other embodied beings. This entails both the way that the speech is uttered via the body (e.g., spoken forcefully while standing over the addressee, as happened to the South Asian boy, Prajay, when trying to play football with the black and white boys) and the ability of speech acts to produce what they name on the body addressed (e.g., repeatedly interpellating the South Asian boys as weaklings effectively renders them so). Butler criticizes Bourdieu for not acknowledging the bodily nature of speech—how it both issues from and impacts bodies. She adds that he also does not see the space between the body and words as one of possible subversion. While Butler grants that speech has a bodily component,[92] my notion of flexible habit makes this bodily dimension more explicit and addresses how the habits of the body itself come to represent what is race or gender insofar as they are circulated and interpreted socially rather than just as linguistic repetition of cultural norms. Butler's work on the potential for linguistic threat and injury through bodily speech acts could offer educators valuable lessons in helping their students become considerate, democratic citizens, sensitive to the potential harm in the language they use and by which they are addressed.

I suggest that a failure of students to dynamically adapt their habitual responses to one another at an important time of racial identity formation, while evident in several of the examples I have depicted so far, is particularly clear in a situation that has occurred in many school cafeterias throughout the country.[93] Beverly Daniel Tatum provides an account of the establishment of the "black table" in the school cafeteria. She writes,

> Not only are Black adolescents encountering racism and reflecting on their identity, but their white peers, even when they are not the perpetrators (and sometimes they are), are unprepared to respond in supportive ways. The Black students turn to each other for the much needed support they are not likely to find anywhere else.[94]

While promoting fruitful group solidarity and at times an appropriately resolute response to racism, this inflexibility in learning to transact across racial difference results in color line division and communication collapse. The development of the "black table" (for which both black and white students as well as the larger social structure are responsible) prevents cross-racial growth. Habitual ways of enacting dichotomy and division begin to sediment.[95]

The notion of transaction can also inform communication within educational settings. Often in schools and elsewhere, distinctions between people are understood as sharp boundaries. Seeing bodies as more fluid and transactional (and teaching of them in this way) could weaken such contrasts and possibly alleviate some of the communication boundaries erected by apparently sharp distinctions of the body—race, gender, age, and the like. Understanding communication as a transactional activity capable of blurring these distinctions and altering the identity makeup of all participants could be an important step for classroom engagements.

Insofar as communication is an activity of making common, it blends the flesh and breaks down discrete identity categories while preserving individuality and avoiding homogenization. The habits of individuals are not smoothed into a dull, shared middle ground through good communication. Rather, those habits that promote communication and preserve uniqueness of individuals are encouraged because they more effectively accommodate the perspectives of all participants and reach a conclusion supported by everyone.[96] Communication as a process of making common negotiates new meanings, including new understandings of gender and racial difference. Within this communally pursued exchange, new vocabularies can be formed, providing new ways to envision relations and to provoke needed alterations of certain stagnant habits. Granted, however, these negotiations may problematically be usurped by the participant who embodies the traditional racial or gender role of privilege. Teachers must be attuned to this possibility and prepared to mediate in ways that not only assuage these inequalities but also effectively call them into question so they can be intelligently confronted by the students themselves. Moreover, teachers should call into question the very *need* for changing inequalities.

CONCLUDING THOUGHTS

Changing one's habits when in communication with others or even over time through one's environmental interaction or educational inquiry changes not only how one transacts but also how one is in the world as well as the world itself. This is a risky endeavor, one made more worthwhile, more rewarding, and more efficient through the cultivation of flexible habits. Flexible habits promote a rethinking and reformation of the more rigid habits that firmly demarcate genders and races or produce problematic responses to difference. They constitute a platform for agency and allow students to have greater impact on the way they enact their identities and respond to others as well as open pathways for introducing larger change in transforming identity and confronting racism and sexism. To close with Dewey, "By a seeming paradox, increased power of forming habits means increased susceptibility, sensitiveness, responsiveness. Thus, even if we think of habits as so many grooves, the power to acquire many and varied grooves denotes high sensitivity, explosiveness."[97] Flexible habits work through dangerous situations, clearing the way for growth and change. Explosive, indeed.

NOTES

1. I am building here off of Gail Weiss, "The Anonymous Intentions of Transactional Bodies," *Hypatia* 17, no. 4 (2002): 188.

2. John Dewey, *The School and Society* (1902; reprint, Chicago: University of Chicago Press, 1990), 80.

3. Marjorie O'Loughlin offers other good examples of embodied educational activity in her "Paying Attention to Bodies in Education: Theoretical Resources and Practical Suggestions," *Educational Philosophy and Theory* 30, no. 3 (1998): 293.

4. John Dewey, *Experience and Nature* (Chicago: Open Court, 1925), 23.

5. John Dewey, *Reconstruction in Philosophy* (1920; reprint, Boston: Beacon Press, 1957), 87.

6. Judith Butler, *Bodies That Matter: On the Discursive Limits of "Sex"* (New York: Routledge, 1993), 8.

7. Dewey, quoted in Shannon Sullivan, "Reconfiguring Gender with John Dewey," *Hypatia* 15, no. 1 (2000): 30.

8. Gail Masuchika Boldt, "Failing Bodies: Discipline and Power in Elementary Classrooms," *Journal of Curriculum Theorizing* 17, no. 4 (2001): 93.

9. Mica Pollock, *Colormute: Race Talk Dilemmas in an American School* (Princeton, N.J.: Princeton University Press, 2004), 27–28.

10. Note that I am not suggesting here a call for the dissolution of identity or loss of the positive aspects of identity as Latino.

11. John Warren further describes powerful words linked to whiteness, including "purity," in *Performing Purity: Whiteness, Pedagogy, and the Reconstruction of Power* (New York: Peter Lang, 2003), 20.

12. Admittedly, Taleshia and April, in particular, may be too young for such abstract descriptions of their activities, but they can still learn about the histories of organizations of prejudice and hate that have used such terms and how repeating them reinforces the beliefs of those communities and may actually be incongruous with their own experiences of cross-racial interaction.

13. Judith Butler, *Excitable Speech: A Politics of the Performative* (New York: Routledge, 1997), 52.

14. For more on the disruption of linguistic injury, see Butler, *Excitable Speech*, 92.

15. Robin Good, "The Blues: Breaking the Psychological Chains of Controlling Images," in *Dismantling White Privilege: Pedagogy, Politics, and Whiteness*, ed. Nelson M. Rodriguez and Leila E. Villaverde (New York: Peter Lang, 2000), 117.

16. Nelson M. Rodriguez, "Emptying the Content of Whiteness," in *White Reign: Deploying Whiteness in America*, ed. Joe Kincheloe (New York: St. Martin's Griffin, 1998), 32.

17. John Dewey, *Human Nature and Conduct* (1922; reprint, Mineola, N.Y.: Dover, 2002), 21.

18. Dewey, *Human Nature and Conduct*, 19.

19. Dewey, *Human Nature and Conduct*, 288–89.

20. Dewey, *Human Nature and Conduct*, 128.

21. Barbara Applebaum, describing Audrey Thompson, in "Social Justice Education: Moral Agency, and the Subject of Resistance," *Educational Theory* 54, no. 1 (2004): 72.

22. Of course, I have said that bad habits have stuck, creating rigid ways of being raced and gendered and hierarchical systems of responding to race and gender. The

difference is that those problematic habits are not the flexible habits that are continually reworked.

23. Charlene Haddock Seigfried, *William James's Radical Reconstruction of Philosophy* (Albany: State University of New York Press, 1990), 294.

24. Note the relationship between thought, habits, and desires discussed in chapter 2.

25. Importantly here, these norms of identity must carefully distinguish themselves from the normalization of identity standards. For more, see Judith Butler, *Undoing Gender* (New York: Routledge, 2004), 41.

26. Dewey, *Human Nature and Conduct*, 291.

27. Michel Foucault, *Power/Knowledge: Selected Interviews and Other Writings, 1972–1977*, ed. C. Gordon (London: Harvester Wheatsheaf, 1980), 39, quoted in Paul Connolly, *Racism, Gender Identities, and Young Children* (London: Routledge, 1998), 14.

28. Judith Butler warns against this in *Gender Trouble: Tenth Anniversary Edition* (New York: Routledge, 1999), xxi.

29. It may even be the case in a strict reading, like that taken by Seyla Benhabib, that Butler's subject is so implicated in the language that constitutes him or her that he or she cannot reflect on or change it. See Seyla Benhabib, "Subjectivity, Historiography, and Politics," in *Feminist Contentions: A Philosophical Exchange*, ed. Seyla Benhabib, Judith Butler, Drucilla Cornell, and Nancy Fraser (New York: Routledge, 1995).

30. Veronica Vasterling, "Butler's Sophisticated Constructivism: A Critical Assessment," *Hypatia* 14, no. 3 (1999): 26.

31. Applebaum also gets at this in "Social Justice Education."

32. Robert Westbrook, *John Dewey and American Democracy* (Ithaca, N.Y.: Cornell University Press, 1991), 442–43, quoting John Dewey, "Is There Hope for Politics?," in *The Later Works of John Dewey*, vol. 6, ed. Jo Ann Boydston (1931; reprint, Carbondale: Southern Illinois University Press, 1997), 188.

33. John Dewey, *Democracy and Education* (New York: Free Press, 1916), 215–16.

34. Applebaum, "Social Justice Education," 68–70.

35. Westbrook, *John Dewey and American Democracy*, 508.

36. Jim Garrison, "A Deweyan Theory of Democratic Listening," *Educational Theory* 46, no. 4 (1996): 441.

37. Elizabeth Dutro, "'But That's a Girl's Book!' Exploring Gender Boundaries in Children's Reading Practices," *Reading Teacher* 55, no. 4 (2002): 379–83.

38. Debra Van Ausdale and Joe R. Feagin, *The First R: How Children Learn Race and Racism* (Lanham, Md.: Rowman & Littlefield, 2001), 123.

39. Van Ausdale and Feagin, *The First R*, 123.

40. Certainly even the best of teachers will not be able to do this for all students or in all cases. The teacher can, however, construct conditions in his or her classroom that get at these habits indirectly and continue to work with the student on developing habits of flexibility that may assist the student in using the conditions to more thoroughly consider or change his or her sedimented habits.

41. Pollock, *Colormute*, 156.

42. Note my early discussion of Paley's work. One might say this causes her to *choose* not to play rather than to be *told* she cannot play.

43. For more, see Megan Boler, *Feeling Power: Emotions and Education* (New York: Routledge, 1999), 180.

44. Dewey, *Democracy and Education*, 49.

45. Butler, *Gender Trouble*, 33 and 140.

46. Dewey, *Human Nature and Conduct*, 102, 103, and 105.

47. Butler, *Gender Trouble*, xxi.

48. Of course, there is the possibility that the teacher him- or herself may not attend to his or her own habits in these ways, making it difficult to model flexible habits or to encourage students to reflect on their own.

49. I cannot help but think here about the classic elementary teacher's "blue eye/ brown eye" experiment and how it creatively explained the lived feeling of prejudice by putting typically racially dominant students in positions of oppression.

50. Dewey, *Human Nature and Conduct*, 20.

51. I note to myself how doing this immediately sounds unethical, yet minority students are often put in isolating circumstances without hardly any notice by those in more dominant positions. I do not know that this fact makes inflicting this experience on a child any more ethically permissible, but it certainly does reveal something about my own sensitivities to the well-being of those in privileged positions and perhaps my underlying desire to keep them there. In addition, moving a white child to a nonwhite space may disrupt some habits of white privilege, but some of those children will continue to maintain a position of power by assuming control of their new space.

52. Jonathan Kozol, *The Shame of the Nation: The Restoration of Apartheid Schooling in America* (New York: Crown, 2005).

53. Charlene Haddock Seigfried, *Pragmatism and Feminism* (Chicago: University of Chicago Press, 1996), 252.

54. Think here of institutional habits of racialized spaces like buses and neighborhoods before the civil rights era and of how desegregation laws and leaders like Martin Luther King Jr. and Rosa Parks helped change the individual habits related to racialized spaces of many Americans.

55. Gert J. J. Biesta and Nicholas C. Burbules, *Pragmatism and Educational Research* (Lanham, Md.: Rowman & Littlefield, 2003), 59.

56. Cris Mayo, "Certain Privilege: Rethinking White Agency," in *Philosophy of Education Society Yearbook*, ed. Chris Higgins (Urbana: University of Illinois Press, 2004), 308.

57. Pollock, *Colormute*, 39.

58. Helen Harper further discusses whiteness as a norm of financial privilege in "White Women Teaching in the North: Problematic Identity on the Shores of Hudson Bay," in *Dismantling White Privilege: Pedagogy, Politics, and Whiteness*, ed. Nelson M. Rodriguez and Leila E. Villaverde (New York: Peter Lang, 2000).

59. Amanda Lewis, *Race in the Schoolyard: Negotiating the Color Line in Classrooms and Communities* (New Brunswick, N.J.: Rutgers University Press, 2003), 56.

60. Megan Boler, "Teaching for Hope: The Ethics of Shattering Worldviews," in *Teaching, Learning, and Loving*, ed. Daniel Liston and Jim Garrison (New York: Routledge, 2004), 119.

61. Applebaum, "Social Justice Education," 59–62.

62. I borrow this description from Mayo, "Certain Privilege," 312.

63. Feagin and Van Ausdale, *The First R*, 61. Please note that I am using this example to envision a more general case of this nature. Admittedly, the children here may be too young to engage in some of the types of conversations and activities I am proposing. Many schools would also likely not permit such politically controversial discussions in the classroom. Robyn M. Holmes also notes how African American children in a kindergarten class are far more sensitive to the nuances of color on their skin and body parts in *How Young Children Perceive Race* (Thousand Oaks, Calif.: Sage, 1995), 49.

64. Shannon Sullivan notes this of her own upbringing in *Revealing Whiteness: The Unconscious Habits of Racial Privilege* (Bloomington: Indiana University Press, 2006), 116.

65. Joe L. Kincheloe and Shirley R. Steinberg, "Addressing the Crisis of Whiteness," in *White Reign: Deploying Whiteness in America*, ed. Joe Kincheloe (New York: St. Martin's Griffin, 1998), 12.

66. Rodriguez, "Emptying the Content of Whiteness," 34.

67. In some ways, this suggestion troubles me. It can seem belittling to the struggles of minority students to suggest that those in the majority also suffer because of racism. The ways in which whites suffer may seem far less significant. Furthermore, highlighting them may make minority students feel as though they lose some ground in their position as those harmed by racism when whites also "invade" that territory as well by similarly claiming harm. I grant, however, that pointing out the costs of whiteness may help white students see problems with their privilege and realize that even though this privilege gains them some goods, it costs them others—including lives that are more full, rich, or ethical when lived in coordination with people of all races.

68. Boler, "Teaching for Hope," 130. One narrative Boler recommends is Minnie Bruce Pratt's essay "Identity: Skin/Blood/Heart," in *Yours in Struggle*, ed. Elly Bulkin, Minnie Bruce Pratt, and Barbara Smith (New York: Longhaul Press, 1984), which depicts one woman's journey through her revelation of complicity in racism to her active efforts to combat it.

69. Boler, *Feeling Power*, 195.

70. American Psychiatric Association, *Diagnostic and Statistical Manual of Mental Disorders*, 4th ed. (Washington D.C.: American Psychiatric Association, 1994): 302.6 Gender Identity Disorder in Children; 302.85 Gender Identity Disorder in Adolescents or Adults.

71. Thanks to Cris Mayo for reminding me of this.

72. Alan Peshkin, *The Color of Strangers, the Color of Friends* (Chicago: University of Chicago Press, 1991), 188.

73. Pollock, *Colormute*, 40.

74. Butler, *Gender Trouble*, 42.

75. Gail Masuchika Boldt, "Sexist and Heterosexist Responses to Gender Bending in an Elementary Classroom," *Curriculum Inquiry* 26, no. 2 (1996): 120.

76. I am responding here to Butler in *Bodies That Matter*, 115.

77. Butler, *Undoing Gender*, 217.

78. Butler, *Undoing Gender*, 236–37.

79. Dewey *Human Nature and Conduct*, 72.

80. Dewey *Human Nature and Conduct*, 161–62.

81. John Dewey, *Experience and Education* (Indianapolis: Kappa Delta Pi, 1998), 70.

82. Dewey, *The School and Society*, 118–19.

83. Dewey, *Democracy and Education*, 141.

84. Butler, *Undoing Gender*, 60.

85. For more on problems with difference as maintaining the norm, see Butler, *Bodies That Matter*, 104.

86. To those who might reply that some classrooms are composed of only one race of children and therefore are incapable of being such a space of difference, I would reply that they have, in large part, failed to understand the types of differences and the trying out of new ways of being that extend beyond the color of one's flesh (if one can even propose such a classification given the arguments in chapter 3) that I have been describing all along.

87. That is until Daniel reverts to rigid, traditional notions of femaleness and sexuality.

88. Dewey, *Experience and Nature*, 141.

89. Here I am drawing heavily on Shannon Sullivan's understanding of habits in communication in *Living across and through Skins: Transactional Bodies, Pragmatism, and Feminism* (Bloomington: Indiana University Press, 2001).

90. John Dewey, *Democracy in Education*, in *The Middle Works of John Dewey*, vol. 9, ed. Jo Ann Boydston (1916; reprint, Carbondale: Southern Illinois University Press, 1980), 12.

91. Sullivan, *Living across and through Skins*, 75.

92. Butler, *Gender Trouble*, xxv.

93. In her school observations, Pollock discovered that racial groups were not so neatly divided at lunch time. She warns, "Still since people analyzing student relations relentlessly described lunchtime as if problematically clear-cut groupings existed, the perception that race would order such student friendships became a matter-of-fact assumption." *Colormute*, 55. I grant that I, too, may make this assumption and fail to see exceptions or other ways in which students organize themselves.

94. Beverly Daniel Tatum, *Why Are All the Black Kids Sitting Together in the Cafeteria?* (New York: Basic Books, 1997), 60.

95. This situation is complicated, however, by the fact that "within the context of solidarity building, whiteness is a set of political, cultural, and social forces linked to relations of domination that have the *potential* to keep individuals and groups from building necessary coalitions that are linked to broader democratic projects. To put it more bluntly: Whiteness in the negative sense is that which separates; it is that which prevents linking particular interests and struggles to the project of a radical democracy." Rodriguez, "Emptying the Content of Whiteness," 59. In this regard, whiteness may prevent the effective establishment of solidarity for democratic ends.

96. Sullivan also ends her call for pragmatic communication on a similar note in *Living across and through Skins*, 81.

97. Dewey, *Experience and Nature*, 281.

Bibliography

Alcoff, Linda Martín. "Towards a Phenomenology of Racial Embodiment." *Radical Philosophy* 95 (1999): 15–26.

——. "Habits of Hostility: On Seeing Race." *Philosophy Today* 44, suppl. (2000): 30–40.

Alemán, Ana M. Martínez. "Identity, Feminist Teaching, and John Dewey." In *Feminist Interpretations of John Dewey*, edited by Charlene Haddock Seigfried. University Park: Pennsylvania State University Press, 2002.

American Psychiatric Association. *Diagnostic and Statistical Manual of Mental Disorders*. 4th ed. Washington, D.C.: American Psychiatric Association, 1994.

Appiah, Kwame Anthony. "The Conservation of 'Race.'" *Black American Literature Forum* 23, no. 1 (1989): 37–60.

Applebaum, Barbara. "Social Justice Education, Moral Agency, and the Subject of Resistance." *Educational Theory* 54, no. 1 (2004): 59–72.

Bem, Sandra Lipsitz. "Genital Knowledge and Gender Constancy in Preschool Children." *Child Development* 60, no. 3 (1989): 649–62.

Benhabib, Seyla. "Feminism and Postmodernism." In *Feminist Contentions: A Philosophical Exchange*, edited by Seyla Benhabib, Judith Butler, Drucilla Cornell, and Nancy Fraser. New York: Routledge, 1995.

——. "Subjectivity, Historiography, and Politics." In *Feminist Contentions: A Philosophical Exchange*, edited by Seyla Benhabib, Judith Butler, Drucilla Cornell, and Nancy Fraser. New York: Routledge, 1995.

Berlin, Ira. "Time, Space, and the Evolution of Afro-American Society on British Mainland North America." *American Historical Review* 85, no. 1 (1980): 44–78.

Bieder, Robert E. "Scientific Attitudes toward Indian Mixed-Bloods in Early Nineteenth Century America." *Journal of Ethnic Studies* 8, no. 2 (1980): 17–30.

Biesta, Gert J. J., and Nicholas C. Burbules. *Pragmatism and Educational Research*. Lanham, Md.: Rowman & Littlefield, 2003.

Bigwood, Carol. "Renaturalizing the Body (with the Help of Merleau-Ponty)." *Hypatia* 6, no. 3 (1991): 54–73.

153

Blumenbach, Johann. *On the Natural Varieties of Mankind*. Translated by Thomas Bendyshe. 1775. Reprint, New York: Bergman Publishers, 1969.

Boisvert, Raymond D. "John Dewey: An 'Old-Fashioned' Reformer." In *The New Scholarship on Dewey*, edited by Jim Garrison. Dordrecht: Kluwer Academic, 1995.

Boldt, Gail Masuchika. "Sexist and Heterosexist Responses to Gender Bending in an Elementary Classroom." *Curriculum Inquiry* 26, no. 2 (1996): 113–31.

———. "Failing Bodies: Discipline and Power in Elementary Classrooms." *Journal of Curriculum Theorizing* 17, no. 4 (2001): 91–104.

Boler, Megan. *Feeling Power: Emotions and Education*. New York: Routledge, 1999.

———. "Teaching for Hope: The Ethics of Shattering Worldviews." In *Teaching, Learning, and Loving*, edited by Daniel Liston and Jim Garrison. New York: Routledge, 2004.

Bourdieu, Pierre. *In Other Words*. Palo Alto, Calif.: Stanford University Press, 1990.

———. *The Logic of Practice*. Palo Alto, Calif.: Stanford University Press, 1990.

———. *An Invitation to Reflexive Sociology*. Cambridge: Polity Press, 1992.

Boxill, Bernard, ed. *Race and Racism*. New York: Oxford University Press, 2001.

Brookey, Robert Alan, and Diane Helene Miller. "Changing Signs: The Political Pragmatism of Poststructuralism." *International Journal of Sexuality and Gender Studies* 6, nos. 1 and 2 (2001): 139–53.

Buffon, Georges-Louis Leclerc de. "Histoire Naturelle." In *Oeuvres Completes de Buffon*, edited by Comte de Lacepède. Paris, 1818.

Burrows, James. *Will & Grace*. Television program. Directed by James Burrows. Studio City, Calif.: NBC Universal Television Studio, 2005.

Butler, Judith. "Sex and Gender in Simone de Beauvoir's *Second Sex*." *Yale French Studies* 72 (1986): 35–51.

———. *Bodies That Matter: On the Discursive Limits of "Sex."* New York: Routledge, 1993.

———. "For a Careful Reading." In *Feminist Contentions: A Philosophical Exchange*, edited by Seyla Benhabib, Judith Butler, Drucilla Cornell, and Nancy Fraser. New York: Routledge, 1995.

———. *Excitable Speech: A Politics of the Performative*. New York: Routledge, 1997.

———. *Gender Trouble: Tenth Anniversary Edition*. New York: Routledge, 1999.

———. *Undoing Gender*. New York: Routledge, 2004.

Chasnoff, Debra. *It's Elementary: Talking about Gay Issues in Schools*. VHS. Directed by Debra Chasnoff. Harriman, N.Y.: New Day Films, 1996.

Clarke, Melissa. "Rosa Parks' Performativity, Habitus, and Ability to Play the Game." *Philosophy Today* 44, suppl. (2000): 160–68.

Code, Lorraine. "Feminists and Pragmatists: A Radical Future?" *Radical Philosophy* 87 (1998): 22–30.

Connolly, Paul. *Racism, Gender Identities, and Young Children*. London: Routledge, 1998.

Darwin, Charles. *The Origin of Species by Means of Natural Selection*. 1859. Reprint, New York: Modern Library, 1936.

———. *The Origin of Species by Means of Natural Selection; Or, the Preservation of Favoured Races in the Struggle for Life*. 1859. Reprint, London: Penguin, 1968.

———. *The Descent of Man and Selection in Relation to Sex*. 1871. Reprint, New York: D. Appleton and Company, 1896.

———. *The Descent of Man and Selection in Relation to Sex*. 1871. Reprint, New York: Modern Library, 1936.

Davenport, Charles B. "The Eugenics Programme and Progress in Its Achievement." In *Eugenics: Twelve University Lectures*. New York: Dodd, Mead, 1914.

Davies, Bronwyn. "The Discursive Production of the Male/Female Dualism in School Settings." In *The RoutledgeFalmer Reader in Sociology of Education*, edited by Stephen J. Ball. London: RoutledgeFalmer, 2004.

Dewey, John. *Outlines of a Critical Theory of Ethics*. In *The Early Works of John Dewey*, vol. 3, edited by Jo Ann Boydston. 1891. Reprint, Carbondale: Southern Illinois University Press, 1969.

———. *The School and Society*. 1902. Reprint, Chicago: University of Chicago Press, 1990.

———. *Democracy and Education*. New York: Free Press, 1916.

———. *Democracy and Education*. In *The Middle Works of John Dewey*, vol. 9, edited by Jo Ann Boydston. 1916. Reprint, Carbondale: Southern Illinois University Press, 1980.

———. *Reconstruction in Philosophy*. 1920. Reprint, Boston: Beacon Press, 1957.

———. "Racial Prejudice and Friction." In *The Middle Works of John Dewey*, vol. 13, edited by Jo Ann Boydston. 1921. Reprint, Carbondale: Southern Illinois University Press, 1988.

———. *Human Nature and Conduct*. 1922. Reprint, Mineola, N.Y.: Dover, 2002.

———. *Experience and Nature*. Chicago: Open Court, 1925.

———. *Experience and Nature*. In *The Later Works of John Dewey*, vol. 1, edited by Jo Ann Boydston. 1925. Reprint, Carbondale: Southern Illinois University Press, 1981.

———. "Is There Hope for Politics?" In *The Later Works of John Dewey*, vol. 6, edited by Jo Ann Boydston. 1931. Reprint, Carbondale: Southern Illinois University Press, 1997.

———. *Logic: The Theory of Inquiry*. In *The Later Works of John Dewey*, vol. 12, edited by Jo Ann Boydston. 1938. Reprint, Carbondale: Southern Illinois University Press, 1994.

———. *Experience and Education*. Indianapolis: Kappa Delta Pi, 1998.

Disch, Lisa. "Judith Butler and the Politics of the Performative." *Political Theory* 27, no. 4 (1999): 545–59.

Dutro, Elizabeth. "'But That's a Girl's Book!' Exploring Gender Boundaries in Children's Reading Practices." *Reading Teacher* 55, no. 4 (2002): 376–84.

Fausto-Sterling, Anne. "Gender, Race, and Nation: The Comparative Anatomy of 'Hottentot' Women in Europe, 1815–1817." In *Deviant Bodies*, edited by Jennifer Terry and Jacqueline Urla. Bloomington: Indiana University Press, 1995.

Fesmire, Steven A. "Educating the Moral Artist: Dramatic Rehearsal in Moral Education." *Studies in Philosophy and Education* 13, no. 3–4 (1994–1995): 169–74.

Fish, Stanley. "Reverse Racism, or How the Pot Got to Call the Kettle Black." In *Affirmative Action: Social Justice or Race Discrimination*, edited by F. Beckwith and T. Jones. Amherst, N.Y.: Prometheus, 1997.

Foucault, Michel. *Power/Knowledge: Selected Interviews and Other Writings, 1972–1977*, edited by C. Gordon. London: Harvester Wheatsheaf, 1980.

Fraser, Nancy. "False Antitheses." In *Feminist Contentions: A Philosophical Exchange*, edited by Seyla Benhabib, Judith Butler, Drucilla Cornell, and Nancy Fraser. New York: Routledge, 1995.

———. "Pragmatism, Feminism, and the Linguistic Turn." In *Feminist Contentions: A Philosophical Exchange*, edited by Seyla Benhabib, Judith Butler, Drucilla Cornell, and Nancy Fraser. New York: Routledge, 1995.

———. *Justice Interruptus: Critical Reflections on the "Postsocialist" Condition.* New York: Routledge, 1997.

Freud, Sigmund. "Remembering, Repeating, and Working-Through." In *The Complete Works of Sigmund Freud*, Standard Edition, vol. 12, edited by James Strachey. 1914. Reprint, New York: Norton, 1933.

Frye, Marilyn. "White Woman Feminist 1983–1992." In *Race and Racism*, edited by Bernard Boxill. New York: Oxford University Press, 2001.

Galton, Francis. *Hereditary Genius: An Inquiry into Its Laws and Consequences.* 1869. Reprint, New York: Horizon Press, 1952.

Garrison, Jim. "A Deweyan Theory of Democratic Listening." *Educational Theory* 46, no. 4 (1996): 429–51.

———. "What a Long Strange Trip It's Been, or, The Metaphysics of Presence: Derrida and Dewey on Human Development." In *Philosophy of Education Society Yearbook*, edited by Lynda Stone. Urbana: University of Illinois Press, 2000.

Gendlin, Eugene T. "The Primacy of the Body, Not the Primacy of Perception: How the Body Knows the Situation and Philosophy." *Man and World* 25, no. 3–4 (1992): 341–53.

Gilman, Stuart. "Degeneracy and Race in the Nineteenth Century: The Impact of Clinical Medicine." *Journal of Ethnic Studies* 10, no. 4 (1983): 27–50.

Good, Robin. "The Blues: Breaking the Psychological Chains of Controlling Images." In *Dismantling White Privilege: Pedagogy, Politics, and Whiteness*, edited by Nelson M. Rodriguez and Leila E. Villaverde. New York: Peter Lang, 2000.

Goodman, Amy. "Justice for the Jena Six." *Aspen Daily News*, July 31, 2007.

Goodwyn, Wade. "Beating Charges Split Louisiana Town along Racial Lines." *All Things Considered*. National Public Radio, July 30, 2007.

Gossett, Thomas F. *Race: The History of an Idea in America.* Dallas: Southern Methodist University Press, 1963.

Gould, Stephen Jay. *The Mismeasure of Man.* New York: Norton, 1981.

Graves, Joseph L. *The Emperor's New Clothes: Biological Theories of Race at the Millennium.* New Brunswick, N.J.: Rutgers University Press, 2001.

Greene, Maxine. *The Dialectic of Freedom.* New York: Teachers College Press, 1988.

Grosz, Elizabeth. *Volatile Bodies: Towards a Corporeal Feminism.* Bloomington: Indiana University Press, 1994.

Halberstam, Judith. *In a Queer Time and Place.* New York: New York University Press, 2005.

Hammonds, Evelynn. "Interview with Evelynn Hammonds." Public Broadcasting System. http://www.pbs.org/race/000_About/002_04-background-01.htm (accessed April 2, 2004).

Haraway, Donna. "A Cyborg Manifesto: Science, Technology, and Socialist-Feminism in the Late Twentieth Century." In *Simians, Cyborgs, and Women: The Reinvention of Nature*. New York: Routledge, 1991.

Harper, Helen. "White Women Teaching in the North: Problematic Identity on the Shores of Hudson Bay." In *Dismantling White Privilege: Pedagogy, Politics, and Whiteness*, edited by Nelson M. Rodriguez and Leila E. Villaverde. New York: Peter Lang, 2000.

Hess, Jared. *Napoleon Dynamite*. DVD. Directed by Jared Hess. Los Angeles, Calif.: Twentieth Century Fox, 2004.

Hoffman, Frederick L. *Race Traits and Tendencies of the American Negro*. New York: Macmillan, 1896.

Holmes, Robyn M. *How Young Children Perceive Race*. Thousand Oaks, Calif.: Sage, 1995.

Hudson, Nicholas. "From 'Nation' to 'Race': The Origin of Racial Classification in Eighteenth-Century Thought." *Eighteenth-Century Studies* 29, no. 3 (1996): 247–64.

Ignatiev, Noel. "Abolitionism and the White Studies Racket." *Race Traitor* 10 (1999): 3–7.

Jones, Alison. "Teaching Post-Structuralist Feminist Theory in Education: Student Resistances." *Gender and Education* 9, no. 3 (1997): 261–69.

Kincheloe, Joe L., and Shirley R. Steinberg, "Addressing the Crisis of Whiteness." In *White Reign: Deploying Whiteness in America*, edited by Joe Kincheloe. New York: St. Martin's Griffin, 1998.

Kohli, Wendy. "Performativity and Pedagogy: The Making of Educational Subjects." *Studies in Philosophy and Education* 18, no. 5 (1999): 319–26.

Kozol, Jonathan. *The Shame of the Nation: The Restoration of Apartheid Schooling in America*. New York: Crown, 2005.

Kuttner, Robert E., ed. *Race and Modern Science*. New York: Social Science Press, 1967.

Lawson, Bill E. "Afterword: A Conversation between Cornel West and Bill E. Lawson." In *Pragmatism and the Problem of Race*, edited by Bill E. Lawson and Donald F. Koch. Bloomington: Indiana University Press, 2004.

Lewis, Amanda. *Race in the Schoolyard: Negotiating the Color Line in Classrooms and Communities*. New Brunswick, N.J.: Rutgers University Press, 2003.

Lewontin, R. C., Steven Rose, and Leon J. Kamin. "IQ: The Rank Ordering of the World." In *The "Racial" Economy of Science: Toward a Democratic Future*, edited by Sandra Harding. Bloomington: Indiana University Press, 1993.

Liss, Julia E. "Diasporic Identities: The Science and Politics of Race in the Work of Franz Boas and W. E. B. DuBois, 1894–1919." *Cultural, Anthropology* 13, no. 2 (1998): 127–66.

Lloyd, Moya. "Performativity, Parody, Politics." *Theory, Culture, and Society* 16, no. 2 (1999): 195–213.

Lorde, Audre. *Sister Outsider*. Freedom, Calif.: Crossing Press, 1984.

Lovell, Terry. "Resisting with Authority: Historical Specificity, Agency, and the Performative Self." *Theory, Culture, and Society* 20, no. 1 (2003): 1–17.

Mayo, Cris. "Teaching against White Agency." Keynote address of the annual meeting of the Mid-Atlantic Philosophy of Education Society, November 2001.

———. "Certain Privilege: Rethinking White Agency." In *Philosophy of Education Society Yearbook*, edited by Chris Higgins. Urbana: University of Illinois Press, 2004.

McClean, David E. "Should We Conserve the Notion of Race?" In *Pragmatism and the Problem of Race*, edited by Bill E. Lawson and Donald F. Koch. Bloomington: Indiana University Press, 2004.

McNay, Lois. "Gender, Habitus, and the Field: Pierre Bourdieu and the Limits of Reflexivity." *Theory, Culture, and Society* 16, no. 1 (1999): 95–117.

———. "Subject, Psyche, and Agency: The Work of Judith Butler." *Theory, Culture, and Society* 16, no. 2 (1999): 175–93.

———. *Gender and Agency: Reconfiguring the Subject in Feminist and Social Theory*. Malden, Mass.: Blackwell, 2000.

Nelson, Lise. "Bodies (and Spaces) Do Matter: The Limits of Performativity." *Gender, Place, and Culture* 6, no. 4 (1999): 331–53.

Nussbaum, Martha C. "The Professor of Parody." http://web.lexis-nexis.com/universe/document?_m=090424c715f3b7645010b78064198140&_docnum=1&wchp=dGLb-Vlz-zSkVA&_md5=87f7298f66 (accessed August 12, 2004).

Oliver, Kelly. "What Is Transformative about the Performative? From Repetition to Working-Through." *Studies in Practical Philosophy* 1, no. 2 (1999): 144–66.

O'Loughlin, Marjorie. "Paying Attention to Bodies in Education: Theoretical Resources and Practical Suggestions." *Educational Philosophy and Theory* 30, no. 3 (1998): 275–94.

Osborne, Peter, and Lynne Segal, "Gender as Performance: An Interview with Judith Butler." *Radical Philosophy* 67 (1994): 32–39.

Outlaw, Lucius T. *On Race and Philosophy*. New York: Routledge, 1996.

Paley, Vivian Gussin. *You Can't Say You Can't Play*. Cambridge, Mass.: Harvard University Press, 1992.

Pappas, Gregory Fernando. "Distance, Abstraction, and the Role of the Philosopher in the Pragmatic Approach to Racism." In *Pragmatism and the Problem of Race*, edited by Bill E. Lawson and Donald F. Koch. Bloomington: Indiana University Press, 2004.

Peshkin, Alan. *The Color of Strangers, the Color of Friends*. Chicago: University of Chicago Press, 1991.

Pollock, Mica. *Colormute: Race Talk Dilemmas in an American School*. Princeton, N.J.: Princeton University Press, 2004.

Pratt, Minnie Bruce. "Identity: Skin/Blood/Heart." In *Yours in Struggle*, edited by Elly Bulkin, Minnie Bruce Pratt, and Barbara Smith. New York: Longhaul Press, 1984.

Rodriguez, Nelson N. "Emptying the Content of Whiteness." In *White Reign: Deploying Whiteness in America*, edited by Joe Kincheloe. New York: St. Martin's Griffin, 1998.

Roediger, David R. *Wages of Whiteness: Race and the Making of the American Working Class*. London: Verso, 1991.

Salih, Sara. *Judith Butler*. London: Routledge, 2002.

Sarich, Vincent, and Frank Miele. *Race: The Reality of Human Differences*. Boulder, Colo.: Westview Press, 2004.

Schiebinger, Londa. "The Anatomy of Difference: Race and Sex in Eighteenth Century Science." *Eighteenth-Century Studies* 23, no. 4 (1990): 387–405.

Seigfried, Charlene Haddock. *William James's Radical Reconstruction of Philosophy*. Albany: State University of New York Press, 1990.

——, ed. *Feminist Interpretations of John Dewey*. University Park: Pennsylvania State University Press, 2002.

——. *Pragmatism and Feminism*. Chicago: University of Chicago Press, 1996.

Smedley, Audrey. *Race in North America: Origin and Evolution of a Worldview*. Boulder, Colo.: Westview Press, 1993.

Stepan, Nancy. *The Idea of Race in Science*. Hamden, Conn.: Archon Books, 1982.

Sullivan, Shannon. "Reconfiguring Gender with John Dewey." *Hypatia* 15, no. 1 (2000): 23–42.

——. *Living across and through Skins: Transactional Bodies, Pragmatism, and Feminism*. Bloomington: Indiana University Press, 2001.

——. "From the Foreign to the Familiar: Confronting Dewey Confronting Racial Prejudice." *Journal of Speculative Philosophy* 18, no. 3 (2004): 193–202.

——. *Revealing Whiteness: The Unconscious Habits of Racial Privilege*. Bloomington: Indiana University Press, 2006.

Tatum, Beverly Daniel. *Why Are All the Black Kids Sitting Together in the Cafeteria?* New York: Basic Books, 1997.

Thompson, Audrey. "Tiffany, Friend of People of Color: White Investments in Antiracism." *Qualitative Studies in Education* 16, no. 1 (2003): 7–29.

Thorne, Barrie. *Gender Play: Girls and Boys in School*. New Brunswick, N.J.: Rutgers University Press, 1993.

Van Ausdale, Debra, and Joe R. Feagin. *The First R: How Children Learn Race and Racism*. Lanham, Md.: Rowman & Littlefield, 2001.

Vasterling, Veronica. "Butler's Sophisticated Constructivism: A Critical Assessment." *Hypatia* 14, no. 3 (1999): 17–38.

Warren, John. "Performing Whiteness Differently: Rethinking the Abolitionist Project." *Educational Theory* 51, no. 4 (2001): 451–66.

——. *Performing Purity: Whiteness, Pedagogy, and the Reconstruction of Power*. New York: Peter Lang, 2003.

Wayans, Keenen Ivory. *White Chicks*. DVD. Directed by Keenen Ivory Wayans. Culver City, Calif.: Sony Pictures, 2004.

Weiss, Gail. "The Anonymous Intentions of Transactional Bodies." *Hypatia* 17, no. 4 (2002): 187–200.

West, Cornel. *The American Evasion of Philosophy*. Madison: University of Wisconsin Press, 1989.

——. *Keeping Faith: Philosophy and Race in America*. New York: Routledge, 1993.

——. *Race Matters*. Boston: Beacon Press, 1993.

Westbrook, Robert. *John Dewey and American Democracy*. Ithaca, N.Y.: Cornell University Press, 1991.

Whitesell, John. *Malibu's Most Wanted*. DVD. Directed by John Whitesell. Burbank, Calif.: Warner Brothers, 2003.

Wilshire, Bruce. "Body-mind and Subconsciousness: Tragedy in Dewey's Life and Work." In *Philosophy and the Reconstruction of Culture: Pragmatic Essays after Dewey*, edited by John J. Stuhr. Albany: State University of New York Press, 1993.

Zack, Naomi. *Philosophy of Science and Race*. New York: Routledge, 2002.

Index

About the Author

Sarah Marie Stitzlein teaches in the education department at the University of New Hampshire. She attended Miami University in Oxford, Ohio, where she received a Bachelor of Arts degree in philosophy with honors. She was also awarded a Master of Education in Curriculum and Teacher Leadership from Miami University. Finally, she earned her doctorate in philosophy of education and women's studies at the University of Illinois. Her primary areas of scholarship are philosophy of education, pragmatism, social justice education, and feminist theory. She has published articles in many journals, including *Teachers College Record*, *Review of Educational Research*, *Philosophical Studies in Education*, *Journal of Gay and Lesbian Issues in Education*, and *Educational Studies*.